DORSET

RICHARD OLLARD
with a Foreword by Christopher Hibbert

A PIMLICO COUNTY HISTORY GUIDE

PIMLICO

An imprint of Random House
20 Vauxhall Bridge Road, London SW1V 2SA

Random House Australia (Pty) Ltd
20 Alfred Street, Milsons Point, Sydney
New South Wales 2061, Australia

Random House New Zealand Ltd
18 Poland Road, Glenfield
Auckland 10, New Zealand

Random House South Africa (Pty) Ltd
PO Box 337, Bergvlei, South Africa

Random House UK Ltd Reg. No. 954009

First published by Pimlico 1995

1 3 5 7 9 10 8 6 4 2

Papers used by Random House UK Limited are natural,
recyclable products made from wood grown in sustainable
forests. The manufacturing processes conform to the
environmental regulations of the country of origin

Typeset by Deltatype Ltd, Ellesmere Port, Cheshire
Printed and bound in Great Britain by
Mackays of Chatham plc, Chatham, Kent

ISBN 0-7126-5197-7

*To Gerald and Una Smith
whose household at Upcot
stands for the character of Dorset life*

Contents

Acknowledgements

The chapter entitled 'Reading about Dorset' makes clear how much I owe to those who have written on this subject before me. The friendship of the late Sir Owen Morshead first introduced me to this delectable county. Days of enjoyment visiting churches and houses all over Dorset in the company of Richard Tyler have contributed to the pleasures of writing. But my greatest debt is to Edward Chaney who read my manuscript with scrupulous care, saving me from many errors and stupidities and enriching it with his own knowledge and sympathy. To them and to other friends who have helped, not least to Heather Godwin who commissioned the book, my best thanks.

Foreword

Lord's Day bells from Bingham's Melcombe, Iwerne
Minster, Shroton, Plush,
Down the grass between the beeches, mellow in the
evening hush.

John Betjeman's delight in the euphonious names of Dorset's villages will be shared by the readers of this delightful book. To Betjeman's favourites – Ryme Intrinsica, Fontmell Magna, Sturminster Newton and Melbury Bubb – there are numerous others to rival them in melodious oddity: Purse Caundle, Owermoigne, Punchknowle, Chideock, Wynford Eagle, Puddletown, Affpuddle, Gussage St Michael, Piddletrenthide, Winterborne Stickland, Okeford Fitzpaine, Sydling St Nicholas. One is tempted to go on, and you *could* go on for a page or more. The names are redolent of the atmosphere of this most lovely, winsome and tranquil of counties; and they carry with them hints of an ancient past.

All over Dorset we are made conscious of this past. There are the Iron Age hill forts, strongholds of a people whose language, manners and traditions remain undiscoverable secrets, Coneys Castle, Lamberts Castle and, most renowned of all such prehistoric monuments, Maiden Castle outside Dorchester, parts of which may date from as early as 3,700 BC. There are the fragments that remain of the Roman town of Dorchester, Durnovaria, capital of the county of the Durotriges; and there is the Cerne Abbas Giant, a figure 180 feet long cut into the chalk of a hill, which some say represents Hercules, manifestly potent, brandishing his huge, knobbly

ix

club. It may perhaps have been at Badbury Rings, the Iron Age fort near Wimborne Minster, that Arthur, the brilliant cavalry leader of the sixth century, won his decisive victory over the invading Saxons, thus gaining a reprieve for the Romano-British civilisation still surviving in the West Country. It was certainly at Wimborne Minster and Sherborne Abbey that early Saxon Christianity was nursed and cradled; at Portland that the first Viking invaders were sighted towards the end of the eighth century; at Corfe Castle, built to watch over the approaches to Poole Harbour, that its châtelaine, Aelfthryth, had her stepson, King Edward, stabbed to death by the men of her household who dragged him from his horse at the Castle Gate in 978; and that, over six centuries later, another châtelaine, Lady Bankes, bravely and defiantly defended the castle walls against the massed forces of Parliament during the Civil War.

This cruel war brought about much suffering and bloodshed in Dorset, the spoliation and destruction of great houses and the decline of Dorset's maritime supremacy and of those once flourishing ports along the coast from Lyme to Poole. Richard Ollard, author of *This War Without an Enemy*, the best short history ever written of the English Civil War, is particularly eloquent about this, explaining how deeply and almost evenly Dorset was divided, some towns, Sherborne and Blandford among them, being strongly Royalist, others, including Weymouth, Lyme and Dorchester, being as staunchly for Parliament. The landed gentry were equally at loggerheads, the Strangways of Melbury, for example, being as determined in defence of the King as the Brodrepps of Mapperton were in support of Pym and Cromwell. Moreover, Dorset lay as a kind of easily overrun buffer state between the rival factions, between the Cavaliers' strongholds in the West Country and those of the Roundheads around London. Consequently, there were repeated clashes here; the fighting was particularly bitter; and the depredations of ill-disciplined and unpaid soldiers on both sides so widespread and merciless that country people formed themselves into bands known as Clubmen to defend themselves against the 'murders, rapines, plunders, outrages and violence' committed by Roundheads and Cavaliers alike.

A parson who lived through these dreadful times, and served briefly as a chaplain in the Royalist army, was Thomas Fuller who had been appointed in 1634 Rector of Broadwindsor between Crewkerne and Bridport. For years Fuller had been collecting materials for his *Worthies of England* in which he wrote that England might be compared to a house and its several shires 'be resembled to the rooms thereof'. With his own room, Dorsetshire, he was unreservedly pleased. It was blessed with 'self-sufficiency of all commodities necessary for man's temporal well-being ... fine wheat, fat flesh, dainty fowl, wild and tame, fresh fish from sea and rivers'. It could 'clothe itself with its own wool and broadcloth made thereof [for] no place in England affordeth more sheep in so small a compass as this country. And as they are provided with warmth in their woollen, so for cleanliness with their linen cloth, great store of good flax and hemp growing therein'.

It can [Fuller added] build its own houses with timber out of Blackmore Forest, and with free stone out of Portland, most approaching that of Normandy in the purity thereof. Nor wanteth it veins of marble in the Isles of Purbeck. And to all this an excellent air, and the convenience of sea, to export for their profit, and import for their pleasure.

Writing almost three and a half centuries after the Rector of Broadwindsor, Richard Ollard, who lives not far from Broadwindsor at Morcombelake, shares his affection for Dorset where, so he tells us, the golden rule is not to be in a hurry. He himself never hurries the reader along. Indeed, far removed from that no doubt apocryphal American tourist who urged her friend not to stop to look at the pictures in an art gallery because if she did so they would never get round it, he assumes a leisurely pace and, in the manner of J. G. Links's *Venice for Pleasure*, suggests that the reader avoids the second-rate so that he can spend more time on the treasures to be savoured. Do not go out of your way to see Shipton Gorge, he advises: it might be worth seeing, as Samuel Johnson said of another place, but not worth going to see; and, should you be intrigued by the name of the village Sixpenny Handley – or as the signpost pointing in that direction has it, '6d. Handley' – do not be seduced into a deviation. 'It is not worth it.'

There are villages enough that are well worth it, many of them with marvellous churches, such as those at Folke and Leweston. They range in period from the Saxon St Mary's, Wareham to the Georgian Gothick church at Moreton, renowned for its windows so delicately engraved by Laurence Whistler to replace those blown out by a German landmine in 1940. The Norman church at Studland is not to be missed; nor the twelfth-century church at Winterborne Tomson, with its charming interior of early eighteenth-century box pews; nor Whitchurch Canonicorum, worthy of its splendid name and containing the shrine of St Candida which miraculously escaped the attention of the furious iconoclasts of the Reformation. The Priory Church at Christchurch, the longest parish church in the country, set in the waterways of a once-important harbour, is, so Richard Ollard suggests, 'one of the most remarkable as well as the most beautiful Norman churches in southern England'. At Winterborne Came, William Barnes, the son of a farmer in Blackmore Vale, was Rector until his death in 1886 and here, moved by the charms of the surrounding countryside and of its people, he wrote those poems, many in dialect, which earned him the title of 'the poet of Dorset' and bring the Dorset scene so vividly to mind:

> By Maycreech hillock lay the cows,
> Below the ash-trees' nodding boughs,
> And water fell, from block to block,
> Of mossy stone, down Burncleeve rock,
> By poplar-trees that stood, as slim
> 'S a feather, by the stream's green brim;
> And down about the mill, that stood
> Half darken'd off below the wood,
>   The rambling brook,
>   From nook to nook,
> Flow'd on below the morning moon.

Two or three miles or so from William Barnes's rectory at Winterborne Came, that other poet of native Dorset stock, Thomas Hardy, was born at Higher Bockhampton; and it is through his novels that the beguiling nature of Dorset will always be conveyed to a far wider readership than the kindly rector ever enjoyed. This, indeed, is 'Hardy country': Nelson's flag-captain, Thomas Masterman Hardy, was born at Portesham. Thomas Hardy's father, a keen musician as well as a builder, played the cello in a band in Stinsford parish church. Hardy himself went to school in Dorchester and as a boy attended such a harvest-home supper as is described in *Far from the Madding Crowd*; as an architect he was engaged on the restoration of several Dorset churches; and, after living for a time in Sturminster Newton and Wimborne, he settled near Dorchester in a house, Max Gate, which he designed for himself. Here he died, never having lost his love for the Dorset landscape nor his power to evoke the changing moods of its open lands, its hills and valleys and, as in this extract from *The Woodlanders*, its woodlands:

They went noiselessly over mats of starry moss, rustled through interspersed tracts of leaves, skirted trunks with spreading roots whose mossed rinds made them like hands wearing green gloves; elbowed old elms and ashes with great forks, in which stood pools of water that overflowed on rainy days, and ran down their stems in green cascades . . . They dived amid beeches under which nothing grew, the younger boughs still retaining their hectic leaves, that rustled in the breeze with a sound almost metallic, like the iron-sheet foliage of the fabled Jarnvid wood.

CHRISTOPHER HIBBERT

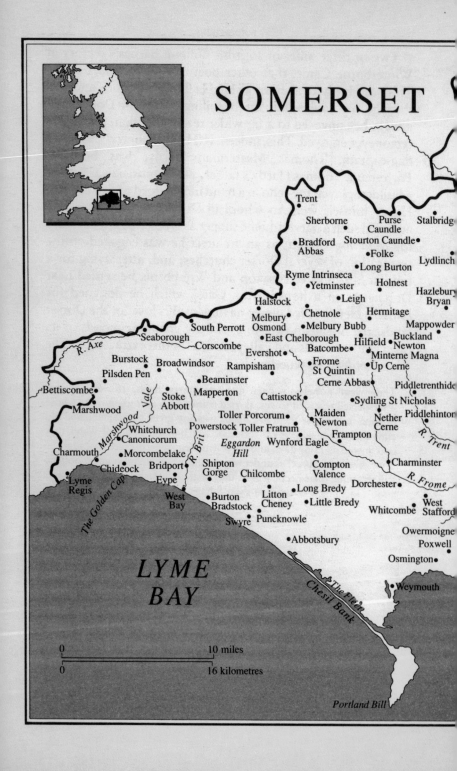

SOMERSET

Trent

Sherborne · Purse Stalbridg
           Caundle
· Bradford Stourton Caundle·
  Abbas   · Folke
          ·Long Burton Lydlinch
Ryme Intrinseca   Holnest
· Yetminster   Hazlebury
         · Leigh   Bryan
Halstock   · Chetnole Hermitage
Melbury   · Mappowder
South Perrott Osmond · Melbury Bubb   Buckland
      · East Chelborough Hilfield · Newton
Seaborough Corscombe   Batcombe· Minterne Magna
           Evershot ·   ·Frome ·Up Cerne
Burstock Broadwindsor Rampisham St Quintin
Pilsden Pen   Cerne Abbas·
         Beaminster   Piddletrenthide
·Bettiscombe· Stoke · Mapperton Cattistock · · Sydling St Nicholas
       Abbott   Nether Piddlehinton
Marshwood   Toller Porcorum · Maiden Cerne
     Whitchurch Powerstock Toller Fratrum Newton
     Canonicorum   Frampton
Charmouth   *Eggardon* Wynford Eagle
   · Morcombelake   *Hill*
 Chideock · Bridport· Shipton   Compton · Charminster
Lyme ·   Eype· Gorge · Chilcombe Valence
Regis   Long Bredy Dorchester·
        West · Burton Litton · Little Bredy   · West
       Bay Bradstock Cheney   Whitcombe Stafford
         Swyre · Puncknowle   Owermoigne
          · Abbotsbury   Poxwell
                  Osmington·

R. Axe

Marshwood *Vale*

The Golden Cap

R. Brit

R. Trent

R. Frome

LYME
BAY

The Fleet

Chesil Bank

0	10 miles
0	16 kilometres

Portland Bill

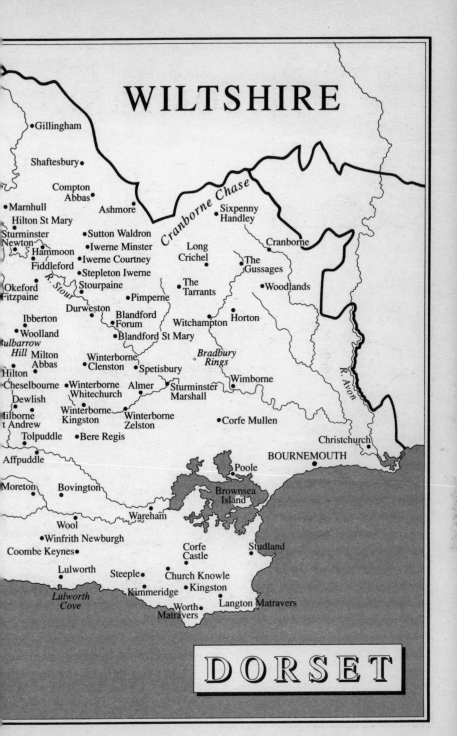

WILTSHIRE

Gillingham

Shaftesbury

Compton
Abbas

Marnhull

Hilton St Mary

Ashmore

Cranborne Chase

Sixpenny
Handley

Cranborne

Sturminster
Newton

Sutton Waldron

Hammoon

Iwerne Minster

Long
Crichel

Fiddleford

Iwerne Courtney

The
Gussages

Stepleton Iwerne

Okeford
Fitzpaine

Stourpaine

Pimperne

The
Tarrants

Woodlands

Durweston

Blandford
Forum

Witchampton

Horton

Ibberton

Woolland

Blandford St Mary

*Bulbarrow
Hill*

Milton
Abbas

Winterborne
Clenston

*Bradbury
Rings*

Hilton

Spetisbury

Wimborne

Cheselbourne

Winterborne
Whitechurch

Almer

Sturminster
Marshall

Dewlish

Milborne
t Andrew

Winterborne
Kingston

Winterborne
Zelston

Corfe Mullen

Tolpuddle

Bere Regis

Christchurch

Affpuddle

BOURNEMOUTH

Poole

Moreton

Bovington

Brownsea
Island

Wool

Wareham

Winfrith Newburgh

Coombe Keynes

Corfe
Castle

Studland

Lulworth

Steeple

Church Knowle

Kimmeridge

Kingston

*Lulworth
Cove*

Worth
Matravers

Langton Matravers

DORSET

I

Dorset: its character

Dorset delights by its differences. It is a county of villages and small towns languidly spread over a countryside that never remains the same for more than fifteen or twenty miles in any direction. There are no big towns – Bournemouth was only wrenched out of Hampshire a few years ago to help with the rates and has no Dorset characteristics. The county has no cathedral. It has no university. It has never fielded a first-class side at county cricket. It hardly has a main through road in spite of the strenuous efforts of the Ministry of Transport to inspire enthusiasm for a trunk road from Folkestone to Honiton – of all improbably desirable journeys.

Yet the last adjective that could be applied to Dorset is dim. It has always counted at every stage of our history and in our pre-history it was without a rival. The large and evidently prosperous civilisation that centred on Maiden Castle just outside the modern Dorchester has left no language, no literature, no political or religious tradition. But the great sites are only now yielding their significance to the archaeologist. Can it be that Dorset owes its special charm to having come down in the world gracefully and without fuss? It would certainly be in character.

Not that one has to be preoccupied with the past to enjoy Dorset. One could equally be mad on hunting or butterflies or wild flowers. No county offers more enjoyment in these departments of life. Its domestic architecture – especially in manors and smaller great houses, in its villages and market towns – is captivating. Its churches range over all the styles from Norman (there is even a Saxon church at Wareham) to the exquisite glass engravings of Laurence Whistler that so triumphantly replace the windows at Moreton blown out by a German landmine in 1940.

It is also the background of the most famous series of novels ever written in the English language and centred on a particular tract of English countryside – the Wessex novels of Thomas Hardy. Hardy was bone of Dorset's bone. His forebears had long been settled in the county as artisans, labourers and small farmers. The cottage at Upper Bockhampton in which he was born is one of the most visited of all the county's attractions. He lived and died on the outskirts of Dorchester and had his wishes been carried out would have been buried there, not in Westminster Abbey. Everyone who has read *Tess of the d'Urbervilles*, *The Trumpet Major*, *The Woodlanders*, *Far from the Madding Crowd* cannot help seeing the landscape, hearing the speech, feeling the weather partly through perceptions so vividly conveyed. His faithfulness to nature is intense. He does not romanticise. Poverty, drunkenness, the harsh struggle of life in a pre-industrial economy set off the beauty of an unspoilt England. There is no rosy glow of universal comfort, no Christmas card effect. In his prose no less than in his verse he is the poet of Dorset.

That title is usually accorded to William Barnes, whose statue presides serenely over the gear-grinding traffic in Dorchester High Street. Barnes, who was born in 1801, and whom the young Hardy knew and admired, is not in the same division of the Poetic League as Hardy but in the strict character of a Dorset as opposed to an English poet he deserves his laurels. Although he wrote verse in standard English his most celebrated and most accomplished compositions are in the Dorset dialect which Hardy used to such effect in his novels. He is represented in the *Oxford Book of English Verse* (the original edition compiled by Quiller-Couch) by a specimen of each variety. No one has ever claimed that he was a genius. But in the gentle tone of his writing as in the even tenor of his long life he expresses the genius of his native county perhaps better than his much greater, much better known, successor. Like Hardy he had few social or educational advantages beyond his long and deep roots in the county he loved. Yet he made himself into a savant of European reputation. Encouraged by his local vicar who lent him books he taught himself French and Italian, Hindustani and Persian and wrote a *Philological Grammar* that established him as a powerful and original scholar. His studies of Welsh and of the Dorset dialect strengthened his preference for the native root-stocks of language over the Greek and Latin influences that formed the new words for the new inventions of the age into which he survived. A farmer's son, he was first a solicitor's clerk before becoming a schoolmaster and, at last, at the age of forty-six a clergyman. In 1862 he was presented to the living at Winterborne Came just outside Dorchester, still one of the most beautiful combinations of great house, park and well-kept parish church in Dorset. He was by all accounts an admirable country parson as well as a learned cherisher of the antiquities in which the county is rich. In the end he became one himself, preserved in the sketch Hardy wrote of him a few days after his death in October 1886.

It is this quality of being loved and valued that gives Dorset its especial charm. The length of its history, and pre-history, has already been remarked. But history, as Gibbon pointed out in a famous passage, is by no means synonymous with happiness. Indeed he asserts that they are antithetical. We are all conscious of places and settings – the Tower of London for instance – where the overpowering sense of the past is anything but benign. Dorset has seen violence and bloodshed in abundance. How could it not? The dominant geographical feature is its long coastline: the sea was where invasion, piracy, pillage would come from. Sir Mortimer Wheeler's excavations at Maiden Castle disclosed one prehistoric massacre and there must have been many more. The Romans, the Saxons, the Norsemen have left civilising traces on a territory they originally entered with fire and sword. As recently as the seventeenth century corsairs from the Barbary ports might descend to pillage, murder and enslave. Even the more civilised forms of warfare with France and Spain might expose coast towns and villages to violence. Yet apart from ruined castles and abandoned earthworks originally erected to deter these incursions the landscape has no overtones of

> old, unhappy, far-off things,
> And battles long ago.

Indeed even these remains seem to have been absorbed into the general tranquillity.

Yet hidden in the county's history are the effects of the most intense of all English political convulsions – the Great Civil War that broke out in 1642. In one respect its effects are still felt right down to our own time, namely in the decline of Dorset's maritime pre-eminence. Right through the Middle Ages the ports of Poole, Wareham, Melcombe Regis, Weymouth and Lyme were thriving centres of trade. With the discovery of the New World in the Tudor age it was these ports that took the lead in the Newfoundland fishery, that great school and source of seamen on which England's seapower was founded. The losses and destruction inflicted on them by the struggle permanently impaired their strength, even, in the case of Melcombe Regis, wiping a once-famous name off the map. This is the most extreme example of the damage. But there were others: great houses such as Abbotsbury and Corfe destroyed, and many, many more stripped of their glories and left but shadows of themselves.

Why was this? Briefly, Dorset suffered from two disadvantages. It was politically fairly evenly divided between Parliament and the King. Of the towns Sherborne, Blandford and Wareham were strongly Royalist, Poole, Lyme, Weymouth and Dorchester Parliamentarian. The landed gentry were by no means solid for the King in spite of the loyalty of such prominent families as the Bankeses, the

4

Strangwayses and the Gollops. Parliament was championed by the Strodes of Parnham, one of whom was among the five members whom Charles I attempted to arrest, by the Binghams of Bingham's Melcombe, the Sydenhams of Wynford Eagle, the Erles of Charborough and the Brodrepps of Mapperton, to say nothing of the Trenchards of Wolfeton. Except for Wynford Eagle which is now a substantial farmhouse rather than a mansion, the great houses of these Parliamentary families still survive; Charborough indeed is still the home of the descendants of its Parliamentary owner. Some parts of England were more or less solid for one side or the other. This meant that the fluctuating fortunes of war caused comparatively little destruction. But where, as in Dorset, the gentry and the towns were divided amongst themselves, the temporary triumph of one side meant a chance of getting one's own back on people who had ruined your house and estate, had smashed your furniture, stolen your treasures, staved the casks in your cellar. Civil wars are proverbially vindictive.

The other disadvantage from which Dorset suffered was that, unlike to-day, it was on the way to somewhere else. Nationally the strength of Parliament lay in the centre and the east – what geographers call the English plain – while the King controlled the periphery, the north, the south-west and Wales. Southern England, perhaps fairly evenly divided in sympathy, was more easily dominated by Parliament because from the outset Parliament gained undisputed control both of London and of the Navy. Dorset thus lay between the Royalists in the south-western peninsula and the Parliamentarians in the south and in London who were likely to march against each other whenever opportunity offered. Nor was this all. The strategy of the Civil War was determined by the possession of strongholds in enemy territory which each side would struggle to reduce (if they were the power locally dominant) or to relieve (if they were the distant power, anxious to maintain a base that could take the enemy in the rear or disrupt his communications).

There were two or three notable instances in Dorset. Corfe Castle was held for the Royalists against hell and high water by its châtelaine, Lady Bankes and Lyme under the inspiring leadership of Robert Blake, the future Cromwellian admiral, defied a much superior force under Prince Maurice, Rupert's brother, in one of the closest sieges of the war. Even writing about it twenty years afterwards Clarendon, the great Royalist historian, exploded with wrath at the 'little vile fishing town defended by a dry ditch' which had inflicted so signal a defeat on the Cavaliers. Portland Castle, though briefly in Parliamentary hands, was almost at once retaken by the Royalists and held out, like Corfe, long after war was palpably lost. Weymouth, which it overlooks, constantly changed hands.

All this meant that Dorset enjoyed no remission from the war. The county was bled white by the exactions of the troops of both sides, themselves almost invariably unpaid and consequently ill-disciplined. Towards the end of the war the exasperated populace rallied to a militant neutralist movement known as the Clubmen:

> If you offer to plunder, or take our cattle
> Rest assured we will give you battle.

Such a slogan had an immediate appeal since it lacked the abstractions of politics and religion for which the war was, in theory, being fought. Its popularity, extending to Devon and Somerset as well as Dorset, of course, presented a serious danger. Both sides exerted all their cunning to seduce the movement into supporting their own cause. On the whole the Royalists seem to have had the better of these negotiations. At any rate Fairfax and Cromwell thought it necessary to destroy the movement by force and did so in a brief action. Naturally these poorly armed men occupied the strong defensive sites of pre-history such as Badbury Rings and Hod Hill. It was here that Cromwell crushed them.

This is not a history of Dorset in the great Civil War – there is already a very good one published more than eighty years ago

(A. R. Bayley: *The Great Civil War in Dorset*, 1910). But the Civil War bulks so large among the influences that have shaped the county that a brief survey seemed necessary. It will echo again.

II
A Survey of Dorset:
The Coast from Christchurch to Portland

The length of coastline in proportion to the size of the whole county is its most obvious physical feature. From Christchurch to Lyme Regis is a transition from an essentially metropolitan world to a defiantly provincial one. It is also a slow, circuitous and various journey.

Christchurch itself, cut off by sensible parking restrictions and pedestrian precincts from its rapidly growing suburban sprawl, is a dignified maiden-aunt of a place. Its pleasant Georgian houses defer in a well-bred way to one of the most remarkable as well as one of the most beautiful Norman churches in southern England. Set in the waterways of a once-important harbour, its great length stretches out as though there were all the room in the world. The richness of Norman exterior ornament is exceptional: but the triumph of the building is its combination of Norman strength and massiveness with Perpendicular light and grace. There is much to admire in the interior: the exquisite chantry chapels, the strong, uncompromising Perpendicular screen, and then the choir, flooded with light, culminating in the splendid fourteenth-century stone reredos in which the free, rhapsodic treatment of the figures is emphasised by their movement behind the strict verticals of their architectural framework.

Of course, one has to admit that Christchurch is only technically a part of Dorset. Historically, like its large western neighbour, Bournemouth, it belongs to Hampshire. But who are we to resist the forward march of bureaucracy? Continuing with our coastal helicopter trip, we find ourselves poised above Bournemouth itself, about the only position from which it might be possible to comprehend its labyrinthine geography. In a car its centre seems always to elude one. Its parts make a deeper impression than the whole. The deep, steep valleys or chines that give it its character are themselves divisive rather than unifying. It has some very good shops and a number of excellent hotels which make it a favourite place for party conferences and other large-scale get-togethers. It has a high reputation in the musical world and supports its own famous symphony orchestra. Holidays and enjoyment, not industry or administration, are its raison d'être.

The soft climate which originally led to Bournemouth's development as a watering-place is also particularly suitable for municipal gardens. These together with a fine spread of late Victorian churches, riding the crest of the High Church restoration of colour and beauty to the public worship of the Church of England, are its great ornaments. If it lacks coherence and design it has a corresponding air of informality, of lack of constraint. It also exudes prosperity. So much of Dorset bears witness to the need for hard work and frugality that has determined the shape and character of what we see that Bournemouth can hardly pass itself off as a native. And why should it? It took no part in the Civil War. Indeed it did not exist until the nineteenth century. It sprang into sudden, thriving life with the construction of the railway from Waterloo. One cannot imagine it offering a setting to any of the Wessex novels, though its recuperative air made it the midwife of two other nineteenth-century classics. Robert Louis Stevenson wrote *Kidnapped* and *Dr Jekyll and Mr Hyde* in Bournemouth where he had been sent for the relief of his tuberculosis.

The views from the beach are beautiful: Hengistbury Head to the east and the Isle of Purbeck; to the south-west, the coast of Studland Bay glimmering across the water, and the hill on which Corfe Castle stands rising behind. One can push along

on the slim Sandbanks peninsula right to the mouth of Poole
Harbour, that roomy inland sea beloved of yachtsmen. The
entrance channel is so narrow that quite big ships can be seen
from close to, always an exciting sight. Just inside the harbour
across another moat-like stretch of water is Brownsea Island,
once the home of the eccentric Lady Houston who financed the
magazine *Saturday Review* and, at one remove, the development of the Spitfire and the Hurricane which saved the country
in the Battle of Britain. She put up the money for a British team
to compete in the Schneider Trophy of 1931. It was won by an
experimental Rolls-Royce plane from which the two fighters
were directly descended. The strength of her patriotism was
such that all the rooms in which she lived were painted red,
white and blue. Brownsea Island is now owned by the
National Trust who have leased a third of it to the Dorset
Trust for Nature Conservation. It is open to the public from
April 1 to October 10 from 10 a.m. till 8 p.m. or dusk if earlier.
Boats run from both Sandbanks and Poole Quay.

Turning back from Sandbanks, a road leads to the left along
the eastern edge of Poole Harbour to the town itself. Poole – old
Poole – is a very different kettle of fish from Bournemouth.
Like Christchurch, it is venerable, and has succeeded in
distancing itself from the docks and multi-storey car parks of
its modern town. As John Newman and Sir Nikolaus Pevsner
pointed out in their excellent *Dorset* this has not been achieved
without grievous losses. But much remains. The Customs
House with its elegant swirling double staircase supports a
porch crowned by the Royal arms. Market Street, High Street
and four or five surviving mansions represent the Georgian age
of Poole's prosperity. But here and there surviving fragments
of medieval warehouses and seventeenth-century almshouses
testify to the length and continuity of its mercantile
importance. Its modern centre has attracted the bustle and
business over which these handsome buildings once gracefully
presided. Both road and railway cross the upper creeks of the
harbour on their way westward. Entering the heathland that is

so characteristic of the south-east of the county they turn south to Wareham, the pleasant little town that marks the western-most reach of Poole Harbour.

Wareham's antiquity is evident from the moment of entry. High above the street on the left hand as you come in stands the simple, beautifully kept Saxon church of St Martin's. There are traces of wall paintings but the most arresting interior feature is the effigy of T. E. Lawrence by Eric Kennington. Lawrence's cottage, Clouds Hill, is only a few miles away, down the quiet lane from which he crashed his huge Brough Superior motor-cycle and was killed. He had got to know this part of Dorset while serving as a Trooper in the Royal Tank Regiment at Bovington, up on the heath above the town. Bovington is still used for training and the Tank Museum is situated there.

The charm of the town lies in its combination of compact-ness with generosity. Still confined within its Saxon ramparts – which you can walk along – it yet seems leisurely and spacious. Partly this is because the seaborne trade that once made it important has long ago departed. As ships grew larger and the approaches silted up Poole drew more and more of it away. But as its elegant seventeenth and eighteenth century buildings show it did not decline into poverty. Now it thrives as a centre for tourism and for the owners of small boats. Both the Piddle and the Frome enter Poole Harbour here and provide the naturally defensible site that the earthworks have improved. Indeed, the Frome forms the northern boundary of the 'Isle' of Purbeck – its western moat is a stream that reaches the sea at Lulworth. It is not really an island at all; but crossing the bridge at Wareham gives you a sense that it is.

The buildings of this most agreeable town are well described in both Draper* and Newman and rightly occupy no less than twenty-three pages of the report of the Royal Commission on Historical Monuments. Its Royalist complexion in the Civil Wars has already been noted. But its royal past stretches

* Jo Draper, Dorset: The Complete Guide. See chapter xv.

farther back. A King of Wessex was buried here in 802. It was evidently of some importance in Roman times and there are some very early Christian inscriptions – seventh and eighth centuries – in the N.E. corner of the nave of St Mary's church, itself the victim of over-zealous restoration in the nineteenth century. It does however contain a remarkable twelfth-century lead font, one of only twenty-nine in England and unique in being hexagonal. The great historian of Dorset, Hutchins, was Rector here for thirty years in the middle of the eighteenth century. The Quay from which boating trips are available exemplifies the tranquillity and graceful proportions of the place.

At this point the railway and the main road to Dorchester part company with the coast, keeping straight on to the west. The Isle of Purbeck, however, juts out to the east and south, looking, on the map, like the head of a belligerent rhinoceros. Nothing could be further from its true nature. A gentle seclusion, protected by the steep range of the Purbeck Hills, calms the most agitated traveller. In any case he has nothing to be agitated about as Purbeck's links with the world of affairs are few. Only its western end, which contains the ruined village of Tyneham, commandeered at a few hours' notice as a battle-school in 1940 and still retained as part of a prohibited military zone, reminds us that even the loveliest places are not immune to the violence of our century.

The northern coast of the Isle forms the southern limit of Poole Harbour, curving round at its eastern end into Studland Bay, whose great stretches of sand offer much the best bathing beach on Dorset's generally rocky and pebbly coast. Part of it is reserved for nudists, and rows periodically break out between the votaries of nature and the ratepayers who like to take the dog for a walk without a full-frontal challenge to their sensibilities. Studland village should help to restore moral and aesthetic equilibrium as it possesses the best Norman church in Dorset, and that is saying something as the competition is stiff.

Still on the east face of Purbeck, between the Foreland and

Peveril Point, opens the smaller Swanage Bay. The coast is characterised by chalk cliffs and caves, with the exciting Old Harry rocks standing close inshore off the Foreland. Swanage itself was the port through which Purbeck marble was exported, but it was never much of a harbour, and the coming of the railway brought the holidaymakers in and carried the produce of the quarries out. Swanage thus developed into a popular resort with a haste that has largely destroyed what must have been a striking beauty of situation. The sea bathing is good and the surrounding country, where the developers have left it alone, attractive. But the pleasures it offers – such as the spirited attempt to re-open the recently closed branch line from Wareham, using steam engines and carriages from the *belle époque* of railway travel – are not specific to Dorset.

The south coast of Purbeck, from Durlston Head past St Aldhelm's Head (its southernmost point) to Lulworth is empty, hilly and of great beauty. This is where the Dorset Coast Path, that wonderful contribution of Enterprise Neptune to the appreciation of history on the hoof, really comes into its own. The road keeps inland. Langton Matravers, which sounds like the aristocratic hero of a 1920s musical comedy, appears at first sight an infiltrated suburb of Swanage, but on a persevering inspection discloses a warm, stony heart. Stone is, of course, very much the local material. The great stone tiles, seen to particular advantage in the village of Corfe, are the hallmark of Purbeck. A detour to the left brings us to Worth Matravers, a notable Norman church and a pretty village. Kingston, back on the main road, is equally attractive. It came into its own late in life when Lord Chancellor Eldon, the statesman of the early nineteenth century who added a new dimension to the word 'reactionary', chose it for his seat. He built a large church, now disused, since his successor, the 3rd Earl, built an even larger one only 300 yards away, a scholarly French Romanesque work by Street.

From Kingston there is a good view of Corfe Castle. The building and the situation make it a winner from any angle.

Perhaps the best view is that coming from the road running westward towards Church Knowle. Its grace is enhanced by the steepness of the hill on which it is set, soaring above the handsome village clustered at its feet. It suggests the heaven-aspiring qualities of a great tower and spire. But its history and purpose are anything but ethereal. Like Wareham it was built to guard the flank of Poole Harbour through which trade flowed and where an invading fleet could ride safely at anchor.

Purbeck in its early centuries was a well-defended frontier zone. The Norman church towers served a military as well as a religious function; at the nearby villages of Steeple and Church Knowle there is hardly a slit, let alone a window, to be seen. Corfe's military history ended, as we have seen, in its glorious defence by Lady Bankes until the Royalist cause itself was lost. Its early history, too, was made memorable by its châtelaine, the terrible Clytemnestra-like figure Aelfthryth, who murdered her stepson King Edward as he dismounted at the castle gate in 978. Edward was rapidly advanced to the status of Martyr and credited with a number of miracles. After an unceremonious interment at Wareham his body was trans-ported to a shrine at Shaftesbury in the north of the county. Corfe remained an important royal castle throughout the Middle Ages. Only in Queen Elizabeth's time was it demilitar-ised. The Bankes family, who bought it not long before the Civil War, remained its owners until they handed over the whole estate, together with that of Kingston Lacy, to the National Trust, in the greatest single benefaction in its history.

Turning south-west towards the coast, the steep ridges of the Purbeck hills tower over charming villages which have kept the compactness that characterises this part of the county in contrast to the rest of it. Church Knowle is perhaps the prettiest and the New Inn looks inviting. But Steeple is even more secluded at the bottom of its valley and Kimmeridge heralds the approach of another famous element of Dorset coast geology to which it has given its name. To the south-east of the village is Smedmore House, one of the most agreeable in Dorset with a beautiful garden. Although in private hands, its owners generously throw it open from time to time in aid of local charities, usually on Wednesday afternoons in summer.

But it is to the west, once the minefields of the military have been negotiated, that the most famous splendours lie. Who has not heard of Lulworth Cove and Durdle Door? No one, unfortunately. In summer the approaches are choked with coaches: caravan sites are everywhere and the unappetising smells of convenience foods fill the air. A sharp, clear day in winter is best for this part of the coast, with its extraordinary rock formations and its amazingly resilient natural beauty.

Apart from smuggling there is little history to this exquisite part of the coast. Over the splendid downs that divide Lulworth from Osmington and Weymouth to the west no road runs. The motorist must turn north, and even slightly east to regain the main road westward. In doing so he should not miss the dramatic shell of Lulworth Castle, all that is left after a disastrous fire in 1929. It was never a proper castle, more a gigantic toy fort completed in the opening decade of the seventeenth century when castles were already things of the past (though the Civil Wars, unimaginable then, were to resuscitate them briefly in the next generation).

The family that have owned it since 1641, the Welds, are still the leading Roman Catholic or recusant family in Dorset. Towards the end of the next century George III, who often came to Weymouth for the sea bathing, was being entertained to dinner at Lulworth. The King, no bigot by nature, was happy to enjoy recusant hospitality. But he was known to have a scrupulous regard for the oaths he had taken at his coronation with their strong and categoric prohibition of civic or political concessions to Roman Catholics. Greatly daring, his host asked him if he would have any objection to his building a Catholic church on his estate. The King, after some consideration, said that he would not, provided that the building did not defy the establishment he had sworn to defend by actually looking like a church. Thus it is that the Catholic Church of St Mary, the first to be built in England since the Reformation, came to look like a charming little eighteenth-century house.

From Lulworth a beautiful wooded road leads to the tiny but extremely pretty village of Coombe Keynes with its thatched cottages and green. It is possible to avoid the overgrown and unattractive village of Wool by taking a by-road to the left and joining the main road at Burton Cross. By this time the landscape has changed to heathland and at this point it is dominated by the nuclear research station at Winfrith Newburgh, lying just to the south of the railway line.

At Owermoigne we enter the rather more genial penumbra of the Dorchester–Weymouth country. There are more trees, and a prosperous-looking agriculture bespeaking a richer subsoil. Owermoigne itself is not so exciting as its name might lead one to hope. There is one much patched-up manor house. But a left turn towards Weymouth only a couple of miles on brings one to Poxwell, a small, neat village with an extremely handsome early seventeenth-century manor house, not open to the public but beautifully maintained, with a charming hexagonal turret-gate to the garden that lies in front of it. In such an exposed position its owner must have shown some quick footwork to have preserved it during the Civil War.

Soon afterwards the road swings west. Osmington is a pretty village where the ruins of another large manor house suggest the possibility of less dexterous or less fortunate manoeuvre. From here it is possible to reach the coast again by a side road to Osmington Mills, a noble site now defaced by caravans but with a fine view over Weymouth Bay. Weymouth itself now spreads out before us. In fact it is the now defunct borough of Melcombe Regis, a prosperous medieval port that returned its own members to Parliament before it was amalgamated with Weymouth to form the eastern end of the town. The front, along which the main road runs, is handsome, unshowy, Georgian architecture, now mostly occupied by unassertive hotels, an appropriate recognition of the homely virtues of the monarch whose wooden statue still presides over the scene. Weymouth – on the seafront at least – has successfully recaptured its eighteenth-century self. Had one come here in the Victorian or Edwardian age, Portland Harbour which lies to the south of the town would have been alive with the great steel-armoured, coal-burning, warships that sustained our empire. The station, now a shadow of itself since the withdrawal of the ferry services to France (though the Channel Islands still keep a ship or two alongside the quay, supplemented by the very successful Condor hydrofoil service) would have teemed with blue-jackets going on leave or rejoining. It is the departure point for one of the most picturesque lines still in operation, the Weymouth to Bristol line, which preceded the coast route to Waterloo. It was down this line through deepest Dorset that Jacky Fisher the Gunnery Lieutenant who was to inaugurate the risorgimento of the Royal Navy, brought Garibaldi to inspect the *Warrior*, that wonderful prototype now happily preserved alongside the *Victory* in Portsmouth Dockyard. Even before the Second World War Portland was one of the Home Fleet anchorages. Now the arrival of a fishery protection vessel would be an event. Till recently the naval helicopters have been based there but soon they too will have gone.

Weymouth features, though not prominently, in Hardy's novels, as Budmouth. Its most recent literary association is with an extraordinarily gifted, passionately reclusive writer, Gerald Edwards, who spent the last few years of his life at no. 654 Dorchester Road. Before his death in 1976, he had finished his great novel, *The Book of Ebenezer Le Page*. Published after his death through the energy of his young friend, the historian Edward Chaney, it won instant acclaim in England, France and America. In form it is a fictional twentieth-century autobiography, set in Guernsey, Edwards' native island.

Portland, though physically separate from Weymouth and

utterly different in character, has been the tail that wagged the dog. Its enormously strong defensive position, an island with steep cliffs and a rocky shore made virtually unapproachable by the strong current, the Race of Portland, that still keeps yachtsmen well out to sea, was made evident in the Civil War. Weymouth changed hands – indeed the Royalist who was appointed Governor, Sir Anthony Ashley Cooper, even changed sides – but Portland Castle remained in Royalist possession from August 1643 to April 1646 when the Governor negotiated very lenient terms of surrender with the Parliamentary admiral, William Batten. The war was then virtually over. Charles I surrendered himself at the beginning of May.

It was off Portland that the first Viking invaders were sighted towards the end of the eighth century. It was off Portland that the early stages of the Armada fight took place. Less than ten years after its surrender to the Royalists it was to witness one of the great victories over the Dutch, won by Blake, the very same man who had inspired the defenders of Lyme Regis against the besieging army of Prince Maurice. Portland was one of the chain of strong points along the Channel coast fortified by Henry VIII against invasion from France. Pushing its great Bill into the sea it looks as if crouched for attack.

The character and accent of the islanders are still said to differ from those of the mainland. No doubt in time past it was even more marked. The way of life and the economy on which it was based obviously differed. Portland was not only an island fortress guarding an important harbour, a kind of Gibraltar of the English Channel. It was also the quarry from which the loveliest stone used in the great buildings of seventeenth and eighteenth century London was exported. Inigo Jones used it for the Banqueting House as early as 1618, and Wren, more famously, for St Paul's half a century later. The expertise in masonry and stone-cutting thus acquired is evident in the island's own architecture, notably in the Church of St George, Reforne, whose architect, Thomas Gilbert, proudly asserts that he is 'of this island'. It is indeed more of a commercial for the Portland stone industry than a place of worship. In spite of its elaborate interior fittings with two pulpits it was only used as a mortuary chapel, apparently, and has long been entirely disused. Naturally it is kept locked up, except in the summer.

The north–south axis Sherborne – Cerne Abbas – Dorchester – Weymouth – Portland roughly marks the division between the landscape of East and West Dorset. Portland will therefore be a convenient point at which to break this survey of the Dorset littoral into two.

III
A Survey of Dorset:
Portland to Lyme

Looking westward along the coast from the height of Portland one sees a feature unique in the whole length of Britain's infinitely various coastline – Chesil Bank and the Fleet. Chesil is an immense barrier of shingle – well over twenty feet high for most of its length and over a hundred and fifty feet broad – which only exceptional storm tides break over. Behind it, the Fleet is a long shallow sea loch whose mouth divides Weymouth from Portland. How Chesil was formed is a geological and hydrographic story beyond the narrative powers of the present writer. Its base is the plasticene-like blue lias which plays such an important part in the geology of West Dorset. On to it the fury of the sea flung hundreds of thousands of tons of pebbles, even rocks, which gradually formed a protective barrier against the very forces that created it. Chesil stretches along the coast as far as Abbotsbury.

Seen from above at either end, it is one of the most arresting natural phenomena of the county, to be compared with the extraordinary rock formations of Lulworth.

Historically its importance was in the grisly trade of wrecking. The Dorset coast is not kind to sailors. Such harbours as there are, of which Poole is the only safe natural one, are never easy to get into and in bad weather impossible. In the days when wind and tide supplied the only motive power, wrecks were common and their produce a welcome addition to an exiguous standard of living. To leave such windfalls to the caprice of nature was not to be expected of unregenerate humanity. Two of the great West Country families who by the seventeenth century had become large landowners, the Strangways of Dorset and the Killigrews of Cornwall, are said to have founded their fortunes in the Middle Ages on wrecking and piracy.

The best image of a storm-driven ship striking on the Chesil Bank is to be found in Meade Falkner's splendid novel *Moonfleet*. Meade Falkner based it on the now depopulated village of East Fleet, virtually destroyed by the great storm of 1824, when the sea breached the Chesil Bank. His account of the smuggling which played so large a part in the life of this part of the country in the eighteenth and early nineteenth centuries is vivid and detailed. Besides his gifts as a novelist and his profession as an armaments salesman, Meade Falkner was a scholar.

The coast road westwards keeps a mile or two inland of the Fleet until it reaches Portesham, a pretty village directly under the steeply rising Downs. The house of Sir Thomas Masterman Hardy, Nelson's Flag Captain at Trafalgar, has survived in its original elegant and unpretentious condition. On the Downs above is a pillar raised in his memory which is visible from most of West Dorset. Slightly to the east of the village on a by-road is Waddon Manor, perhaps the most beautiful of the many small country houses in Dorset. It was built in the second half of the seventeenth century by a friend of Pepys, Colonel Bullen Reymes. Reymes shared Pepys's passion for the theatre. Like Pepys too, he was a skilled musician and formed a fine library. He also had professional dealings with him at the Navy Board over the supply of cordage and sailcloth. This was very much a West Dorset industry – the best hemp in England was grown between Bridport and Beaminster. Reymes, who had been a Royalist in the Civil War and had suffered for it, went into partnership with a Parliamentarian family in Weymouth, the Pleys. Mrs Pley was a particularly good businesswoman, one of three whom Pepys regularly dealt with. Like Pepys, Reymes was both a Fellow of the Royal

Society and a Member of Parliament. It is good to think that so useful and civilised a life and so charming a house should rise from the ashes of the Civil War. Waddon is not open to the public but it is still lived in by a collateral descendant of Reymes and the house is set right on the road so that its grace and beauty can be appreciated by anyone who comes to look.

Leaving Portesham the road twists seaward to the strikingly lovely village of Abbotsbury. The long street of orange-gold stone cottages, all well-thatched, would seem a perfect setting for the old English life of farm labourer, blacksmith and country craftsman. The denizens are in fact unlikely to be horny-handed sons of toil, and the main economic activity centres on the tourist season during which the place can become crowded.

Historically, as its name asserts, it owes its importance to the rich abbey of which the only surviving evidence is the noble tithe barn into which its fruits were gathered. The abbey was at the eastern end of the village. It was of ancient foundation and even before the Norman Conquest notably well endowed. By the time of the Reformation it owned land all over Dorset and even some in Wiltshire. Such wealth was proverbially the foundation of many famous families.

> Hopton, Horner, Smyth and Thynne,
> When abbots went out, they came in.

In this case the beneficiaries were the family of Strangways. Already they had it seems developed a special relationship with the abbey before its suppression. One of them had married the Abbot's sister and a plaintive letter from one of the monks preserved at Westminster Abbey suggests that the loss to the county's devotional life was not severe. At any rate, the Strangways family moved into the abbey and converted it into their country seat.

In the Civil War they took the Royalist side and raised a regiment for the King. In October 1644 Sir Anthony Ashley Cooper, who had changed to the Parliamentary side after a squabble about his Governorship of Weymouth, appeared at the head of a large force before the house (which abutted on the church) and demanded its surrender. The Strangways contemptuously refused and 'hung out the bloody flag'. The fight that ensued was extremely fierce. After the church had been stormed by the attackers, terms were again offered, with the grim warning that if they were not accepted no quarter would be given. The defenders remained defiant. But after six hours' close action the attackers succeeded in piling furze against the house and firing fireballs into it. The house became an inferno and cries for quarter were heard, to which the future Earl of Shaftesbury (and founder of the Whig party) sternly refused mercy. However, the forces on the western side of the house, commanded by Colonel Sydenham of Wynford Eagle, proved more humane and accepted the surrender of Colonel Strangways, three or four officers and a hundred and thirty men. Ashley Cooper's troops, intent on plunder, rushed into the blazing house in spite of his warning that the flames might soon reach the Royalist magazine. This in fact happened, adding to the already considerable carnage.

So complete was the destruction that the Strangways never attempted to rebuild the house, moving instead to their other house at Melbury. Intermarrying with the family of Fox in the reign of Charles II they added the name to their own and were created Earls of Ilchester. It was a later Earl who laid out the famous tropical garden, just to the west of the village, and the much visited swannery. Both owe their location to the Fleet, on which swans had been abundant in the Middle Ages, and whose proximity to the gardens produces a micro-climate in which, even during the coldest winters, frost is virtually unknown. They are open from the middle of March to the middle of October. Always beautiful, they are at their most spectacular in spring.

This by no means exhausts the attractions of Abbotsbury. The serenity of the parish church with its handsome Georgian east end, so unexpected and yet so harmonious in this light, late Gothic building, seems worlds away from the fearful scenes of the Civil War, though its Jacobean pulpit preserves the bullet holes of the Parliamentary attack. It was in this church that the aging Hardy stood godfather to the child of John Middleton Murry in 1925. Murry had defended Hardy's novels from the criticism of George Moore. The poet invited him down to Dorset and took him to Chesil Beach where Murry saw, and was at once enchanted by, the old coastguard station, then disused and empty. It came up for auction a week later and on impulse Murry bought it for £925. He only had £200 in the world but to his astonishment a few days later he received a cheque for £1000, royalties on the books of his first wife Katherine Mansfield. She had never earned anything like that in her lifetime. The coincidence he took as her blessing on the second marriage he was then contemplating as well as on the house in which his son was to be born.

To the south, on its own hill, stands St Catherine's chapel, preserved at the Reformation because of its importance as a sea-mark. The view, no less than the building itself, is worth the climb. On the landward side, to the north-east, a narrow winding road climbs up the steep downs in the direction of Hardy's monument. Not far out of the village to the left a footpath leads to the prehistoric stone cromlech known as The Grey Mare and her Colts.

From Abbotsbury going westwards, the road turns inland just after the lane leading to the gardens, and climbs very steeply to the top of the downs along which it bounces and twists with splendid views out to sea and along the coast. In summer there is a great deal of traffic, so that the distractions of natural beauty can prove hazardous. Clinging to the seaward side of the hill is the small hamlet of Bexington which has never recovered from being sacked by the French in 1440. Its church was never rebuilt; instead, more than two centuries later, its remains were transported to form the south chapel of the parish church of Puncknowle, about a mile to the north of the road. Puncknowle is a charming secluded village with a particularly interesting church. There are several Norman features – the tower, chancel arch and font – and, as you go in, a splendid monument to the Napier family quotes Pindar at you. The Napiers were another Royalist family who suffered for their activity but evidently recovered enough to erect this sumptuous piece.

The little village of Swyre, directly on the road, consists of a large pub, a church and a large rambling house, no doubt once the rectory, in which the distinguished and delightful man of letters Christopher Sykes and his wife Camilla, whose eye for gardens and for domestic interiors was justly admired, spent their last years together.

Along this part of the coast there are a few beaches from which bathing is not made penitential by sharp stones and prickly beds of gravel. Demand, however, is apt to exceed supply and a stiffish parking fee may be exacted. Solitude is hardly to be expected. On the other hand here, as nearly everywhere in Dorset, walking and riding through beautiful country offers all the solitude one could want. Footpaths and bridleways are generally well marked and the country roads, though well surfaced, are essentially survivals of these earlier forms of locomotion. Round any blind corner there may be a girl on a thoroughbred or a senior citizen taking his dog for a walk.

But we are still on the busy coast road to Bridport, approaching the pretty village of Burton Bradstock, whose street plan was certainly not conceived with the motor car, let alone the articulated lorry, in mind. It has an extremely handsome church down a quiet side street. Do not be deceived by a signpost pointing to Shipton Gorge. This is not Dorset's answer to the Grand Canyon but a village whose squires rejoiced in the surname of Gorge (one of them was badly wounded in the action at Abbotsbury in 1644). It is in fact a pleasant enough place but hardly warrants a detour.

Bridport now begins to make its presence felt. There are caravan sites. There is a golf course. For some time now the dramatic shape of the Golden Cap, so called from the bright layer of sand at its summit, has dominated the distant view of the coast. It lies five miles the other side of Bridport and is the highest hill on the whole Channel coast. Bridport itself has not for two or three centuries been on the sea from which it took its name and long earned its livelihood. But it has its own port, called West Bay, to which you can turn before entering the town. West Bay is very much a fisherman's and, secondly, a yachtsman's port. It has an excellent fish restaurant on the inner harbour (The Riverside Restaurant), a hotel which buys its fish fresh from the day's catch (The George), a fish shop (opening hours varying with the seasons) which owns its own boat (The Trawlerman), and some picturesque sheds open all the year round where fresh fish other than the local catch can be bought. Fish and yachting are West Bay's raison d'être. There are some seaside amusements available but its heart isn't in them.

Bridport itself, by contrast, combines its functions as a small market town with a readiness to provide for, indeed to welcome, the visitor on whom its prosperity largely depends. There is a pleasant little Museum in South Street which sensibly concentrates on the history of the town and of the industry, still modestly flourishing, for which it has been known since the Middle Ages, that of rope and net making. The fields of hemp on the road to Beaminster that Fuller admired when he was Rector of Broadwindsor in the seventeenth century have long given way to ordinary crops. Net-making from artificial fibres, rather than cordage for ships and darker uses is the twentieth-century staple. Fuller records the traditional witticism 'stabbed with a Bridport dagger' to indicate that the person so described had had the misfortune to be hanged. Rope making, as can still be seen in the great ropehouse at Chatham Dockyard, requires long 'walks' as they are called to allow the great skeins to be twisted up into a cable that will stand the strains of fierce winds and seas. Evidence of these can still be seen in the long alleys that stretch back from the houses fronting the streets of Bridport. And what streets! There are several stone buildings in Bridport. If you come in from West Bay or Burton Bradstock past the brewery where excellent beer is still made (Palmers I.P.A is one of the best in a county where standards in these matters are high) you come almost at once to a conspicuous medieval building known as the Chantry. What it was built for, or even when, is far from clear. It does not look much like an ecclesiastical building as its name implies. But it shows, uncompromisingly, that Bridport was a substantial place in the Middle Ages.

For the rest the street, broadening with an unservile deference before you, shows the characteristic mix of brick-work and softly coloured stucco that makes the town a perpetual delight. On the left, set back from the road, is another stone building, the parish church of St Mary, a confident, cruciform, perpendicular building with a central tower and a fine peal of bells. Dignified and not in any way individual it represents the settled prosperity the town had already achieved by the time of the Tudors. In fact, the two western bays of the nave were added in Victorian times. The porch is handsome and the Rectory across the churchyard from it is still, exceptionally in this Maoist age of the Church of England, the Rectory.

Further up the street on the right, the medieval stone porch of what is now the Bridport Museum juts agreeably out on to the pavement. There is plenty of room. Even on market days when the stalls are up on both sides of South Street and of the two arms that cross the stem of its 'T', West Street and East Street, one is not crowded. The breadth of the streets and the absence of tall buildings keep everything on a human scale. Walking about Bridport, it is impossible to think about the Public Sector Borrowing Requirement, or the velocity of currency circulation.

The centre of the town, long in view as we make our way up South Street, is the Town Hall, graceful, unshowy and beautifully proportioned. Its agreeable little cupola is a conspicuous feature if you look down on the town from any of the charming hills that surround it. Like everything else here, it doesn't take itself too seriously. The ground floor is taken up with a butcher's shop, entered from the arcade on the corner of East Street.

Slowly, the deposit of late twentieth-century urbanism is silting up the stream of an old market town. There is no longer a saddler. The last corn-chandler's shop, full of pleasant smells not easily defined but somehow suggesting leather, with open sacks of hoof-and-horn meal and other pre-industrial ferti-lisers, closed a few years ago. In their place the off-licences that you would see in Wimbledon or Woking seduce you with special offers of Chardonnay and Cabernet Sauvignon from different parts of the globe. There are a multitude of cafés and bakeries, plenty of butchers, a sprinkling of greengrocers, and some inviting pubs and hotels where the food is generally very good. In both directions, east and west, the street falls gently downhill to the two little rivers, the Brit and the Asker, whose confluence shaped the site. There are a number of handsome buildings, well described by both Newman and Draper. The Unitarian Church, set well back from East Street, has an exterior of great charm. The Arts Centre in South Street is imposing. There is a good new bookshop in South Street and, across the road, a very reasonable second-hand one. The alleys and arcades that run back from the main streets are nearly all rewarding and give you sudden, unexpected glimpses of the totality. And there *is* a totality. Bridport may be under siege from the deadening, homogenising forces of the late twentieth century but it is putting up quite a fight.

Which is more than it did in the Civil War, when it shared with Dorchester a reputation for ignominious surrender to whatever force, however inferior, that might demand it. Moving westwards we reach the most bitterly contested part of the county in that great struggle. Lyme's defence was one of the pivots on which the war turned. But before we get there, indeed the first village we come to on the main road, is

Chideock, which was as staunchly Royalist as Lyme was Parliamentarian. There were two causes of this. The Arundells who were lords of the manor from the Middle Ages to the time of Queen Victoria were firmly recusant; indeed, they were the leading recusant family of West Dorset, as the Welds were of the East. (Interestingly, they were succeeded in the nineteenth century by another branch of the Welds, so that the religious complexion has remained unchanged). Such continuity of tenure generally meant that people living on the estate adhered to the same profession of faith, and this was certainly the case at Chideock. And Roman Catholics were almost by definition Royalist. Moreover Chideock, situated where the road to the west twists through the coastal hills, had from early times been recognised as occupying an important strategic position. A large castle had been built there which was of course at once garrisoned for the King. Charles I spent a night there during his successful western campaign in the early autumn of 1644. It was a most impressive building as can still be seen from the views of it taken shortly before its demolition in the following century. Just how good the masonry was can be seen today in some of the houses that front the street in Chideock and in many of the farm buildings within a radius of several miles. The stone came from the hill just above, still called Quarr Hill though no one cuts stone there now.

The proximity of these two strongholds, Chideock and Lyme, meant that anyone living in between had a pretty thin time of it. If you yielded to the threats of one side, let alone if you actually sympathised with it, you would be punished by the exactions and depredations of the other.

Chideock, now somewhat dazed by the traffic pouring through, remains a pretty village. Climbing up the hill to the west with Langdon Hill and the Golden Cap to the left (there is an N.T. car park hidden among the trees of Langdon Hill and a level, contour-following, path round it beloved of senior citizens) the motorist catches a brief glimpse of the most rural, sequestered valley of the whole county, the Marshwood Vale to which we will return. A mile further on, the road slides down the southern shoulder of the Char Valley towards Charmouth (clearly visible from its by-pass).

Charmouth is rather prettier than Chideock, climbing up its cliff at the foot of which is a beach which has a good stretch of sand. There are a number of handsome pubs, at one of which, the Queens Arms, the young Charles II spent an anxious night in September 1651 when he was on the run after his crushing defeat at Worcester. A bargain had been struck with the master of a coasting vessel who would take him across to France. The long-boat would be off the beach at midnight. The King and his attendant slipped out in good time. But no boat came. What had gone wrong? In fact the ship-master's wife, knowing that he had no cargo and suspecting that he might be going to do something that would land him in trouble with the authorities, had locked him in his room when he had come home to pack his sea-things. The King, of course, had no means of knowing this. As the sky began to pale it became clear that his plan had been compromised and that he must be in acute danger. His escort got him away, first to Bridport, where suspicions raised by the blacksmith at Charmouth nearly led to his capture, and then, by an inspired deviation inland, to Broadwindsor and, ultimately, to his original safe house at Trent in the extreme north of the county. For a fuller account of this story the reader is referred to the present author's *The Escape of Charles II*.

Before following the steep, wooded, sharply twisting road to Lyme it might be convenient to say something of the coast path west of Bridport, which may be reached either from the small and snug village of Eype (pronounced to rhyme with sheep) or from Eype beach, itself a much-favoured bathing place. From Eype itself there is a track up to Down House, from which a short detour to the north brings you to the top of Eype Down (itself part of the N. T. estate) with magnificent views in all directions. Bridport lies below you to the east and on the skyline slightly to the north and east of Bridport stands the silhouette of Eggardon, sheerest and most dramatic of all the West Dorset hill forts. To the north of that again is the long array of W/T masts from which the World Service is transmitted, just above the village of Rampisham. Due north, almost, if you continue along the track and cross the main road above Chideock you can follow Quarr Lane, past Quarr Hill, until it brings you down into the Marshwood Vale between Whitchurch Canonicorum and Shave Cross. If there has been any rain this will be very muddy and though passable even on a horse there are places where the briars hang down to scratch you if you do not keep a good look-out.

Looking westwards you see the tumble of the hills along which the path will take you, with the Golden Cap towering over them all. On a clear day – or more accurately in a clear light, since cloud and sea-fret give way to piercing clarity and then return again with unpredictable suddenness – you can see the whole coast-line of Lyme Bay curving away to your left until it ends at Start Point. Coming down towards Down House and the coast path you will see to the south-east Portland pushing its bill into the sea to form the opposite limit of the bay. It is an exhilarating place to be. At almost any season except the dead of winter there are butterflies about, in some profusion, and the wild flowers have not suffered from the chemicals of modern farming. In the spring the great drifts of bluebells under the trees, with the dazzling white of wild garlic and the pinkish crimson of the campion that lasts the summer through, carpet the ground with colour.

Past Thorncombe Beacon, again with wonderful views across the Marshwood Vale inland and seaward over Lyme Bay, the path begins to descend quite steeply towards the pretty little hamlet of Seatown, till recently nothing but a row of fishermen's cottages and a well-set pub, the Anchor, with a terrace protected by the hill behind on which it is often warm enough to sit out in winter when the sun is well up. The recent development of two large caravan sites can hardly be said to enhance the beauty of the scene. But Seatown has an easily accessible beach on which there is usually some sand to be found.

Refreshed, the coast-path walker faces a steep climb to the path that skirts the southern slope of Langdon Hill and crosses the grassy saddle between it and its grand, bare neighbour, the Golden Cap. From here the views across to the western end of the Marshwood Vale, to the hills of Pilsdon Pen and Lewesdon are again glorious. And ahead, slightly to the right, is the first view of Lyme itself with the Cobb jutting daringly but not altogether confidently out to sea. The path down the western flank of the Cap is constantly changing its route as the coast here is much subject to erosion. On a sunny day you can see through the clear blue water the dark foundations of those parts of the hill that have fallen into the sea. It is dangerous to walk under these cliffs and idiotic to attempt to climb them or to lower yourself over the face. The stratum of blue lias forms a non-porous base over which the sea-water, forcing itself in at high tide, runs out again carrying with it the soil that supports the cliff above. Hence these unpredictable falls, hence the jumble of fallen-in cliff, known as the undercliff, which lies between the cliff proper and the beach. The undercliff again is strictly to be avoided: it is full of adders, and the layers of blue lias are treacherous and retentive. When cows blunder into it they cannot always be got out and when they can it is a difficult and dangerous job. The farm between the Cap and Westhay, a mile-and-a-half as the crow flies, loses about two acres a year of its land to the undercliff.

This constant stirring of the geological structure is of course the main reason why this coast has provided so many and such sensational fossil specimens. There is a museum of them at Lyme Regis but the most exciting ones are, naturally, in the national collections. A further consequence of this instability is that it is almost impossible to get down to the beach between Seatown and Charmouth. Starting from either of these places, it is perfectly possible at the right tide to walk along keeping far enough out to avoid cliff falls. But the only direct access between these two points is a rather dodgy path and then down some even dodgier and very slippery steps cut in the cliff at the now deserted village of Stanton St Gabriel, immediately to the west of the Golden Cap. The National Trust very sensibly utter warnings and disclaim responsibility for any mischance that may befall the too rash beach-seeker. It is better not to try this unless you know exactly what you are doing.

A deserted village stirs the imagination, the more so if it has so grand a name as Stanton St Gabriel. All that is visible is a substantial brick and stone thatched farmhouse, skilfully converted by the National Trust into four holiday cottages, one privately owned whitewashed cob and thatch cottage, and the ruins of a small church in which the Holy Communion is still celebrated on Ascension Day. There are suggestive lumps alongside the track leading towards the cove (whose difficulty of access has been mentioned) but the site has not been excavated nor is there any reason to think that anything much would be found if it were. In 1650 there were still twenty households but the village was probably abandoned by the end of the seventeenth century. Probably the change in ecology and in the conformation of the coast caused by erosion destroyed what can only have been a slender economic base. But the name lingers on. Morcombelake, which straggles along the main road, is happy to count itself part of the parish of Stanton St Gabriel, which also includes the two great hills of Stonebarrow and Chardown from which there are splendid views of the same kind as from the Golden Cap. They are easier of access as there is a narrow twisting lane (itself of great beauty at all times of year) leading up from Charmouth to the National Trust car park on top of Stonebarrow.

Charmouth itself has already been described. The last lap of the Dorset Coast Path leading to Lyme has itself suffered considerable erosion so that officially you are advised to go inland of Lyme Golf Course. Should you prefer to go by car a more than usually generous ration of right angle turns and sharp curves that never end when you expect them to will lead you to think that you will soon be back where you started. But a sudden final twist leaves you poised almost vertically above Lyme. You can hardly see the town except those bits of it that front the sea. It is the sea, in all its immensity, that stretches out below you. As you begin a gingerly descent, you may regret the ugly developments that spoil the effect and impair your view. Lyme never had much room, crammed in at the foot of its steep hills with the sea, in rough weather, crashing into its front. Its narrow, steep streets are, appropriately enough, like gangways and ladders aboard ship. No space is wasted and it is that that gives it its style and its charm. The middle-aged spread permitted on its approaches is out of character.

And there, down at the bottom, it still is. There are good shops and restaurants and pubs and hotels. The coach trade is catered for as much as the more delicate taste of the young ladies from Uppercross. Lyme, indeed, is more conscious of its literary than its historic antecedents. The cottages along the front are named after characters out of *Persuasion* and you will not easily be allowed to forget that the Cobb was not only the scene of Louisa Musgrove's mishap but the stamping ground (if such an expression may be permitted) of the French Lieutenant's Woman. Her creator is himself a public-spirited resident of the town who has done all he could to preserve it from the ravages of development and has written a good local history.

The views from sea level back along the range of cliffs to the Golden Cap are notable. But it is the disintegration of the coast that gives Lyme its special claims to fame, namely the Fossil Museum and the curious dark (indeed to some depressing) walk along the undercliff (here safe from adders and other dangers) to Axmouth six miles away from which there is no egress, except by turning back or pressing on to the bitter end. Since only the first couple of hundred yards or so are in Dorset it falls outside the scope of this work.

IV

West Dorset:

the hinterland

Counties seem to lend themselves to threefold division. The greatest of them, Yorkshire, got on perfectly well without a South Riding until the bureaucrats invented Humberside, a concept as bogus as it sounds with no roots in history, sentiment or trade. Dorset, apart from its coast already surveyed, could really manage with just East and West. But the heathlands to the south-east are not obviously related to the rest of the East and so might qualify for a third division. Perhaps two and a half might be nearer the mark. Anyway, West Dorset has no doubts about its own identity.

Its landscape is emphatically that of hill and valley rather than of broad, sweeping plain. Its climate is generally wetter and milder than the east. It is on the whole better wooded. Certainly, it is fortunate in its woodlands which enhance its beauty with beech and oak and ash, but its great hills and downs are as a rule bare and astonishingly rectilinear in outline. The great south-westerly gales have planed them down. Here and there some of the old hill forts, such as Coneys Castle and Lamberts Castle overlooking the Marshwood Vale, carry a thick covering. And Lewesdon Hill to the east of them surges and heaves in a gale like the sea itself. But, characteristically, the hilltops look as if they had been finished off with a carpenter's rule: the Golden Cap, Eggardon, Waddon Hill, Lewesdon's southern neighbour.

Eggardon might perhaps be classified as a work of art as much as a wonder of nature. An Iron Age fort of the same period as its neighbours, Coneys Castle and Lamberts Castle, and its far greater cousin Maiden Castle, it commands the most beautiful complex of views, differing as you turn along its ramparts, from any site in Dorset. It is still magically unspoilt. The tarmac of car parks, the roughcast of toilets, the assertive smell of burgers too richly garnished with fried onions, that so often certify the proximity of some jewel of the nation's heritage are blessedly absent. Dorset's informality, its unaffected rusticity, has been allowed to heighten the pleasure of your visit. Whichever way you come to it the approach is delightful. Coming from Bridport, the road winds up a hillside free from human habitation except for the enticing and conveniently placed Spyway Inn. Coming from Dorchester, the narrow ribbon of a Roman road runs straight for miles along the top of a great ridge until just short of Eggardon it begins to jink into a right-angled turn or two and you see the fort suddenly rising up on your left. If you leave it there and carry on for a quarter of a mile you come to a signpost pointing in two different directions to Maiden Newton. If you take the one to the right you come at once to a delectable picnic area. And if you persist down that road you find yourself zig-zagging down an almost vertical hill to Wynford Eagle, itself gratefully preserved from the intrusion of the twentieth century. A couple of cottages and a rather bedraggled early nineteenth-century church (which still gallantly soldiers on in the absence of any visible source of congregation) are the only architectural retainers of what was once the seat of one of the great Dorset families, the Sydenhams, who took the Parliamentary side in the Civil War. Their fine stone manor house is still crowned by the Eagle that commemorates a Norman family that left its name to the village. Colonel Sydenham, it may be remembered, showed mercy to the Strangways and their followers at the storming of Abbotsbury. He had not always shewn such humanity, having provoked savage Royalist reprisals by hanging six prisoners of war on the grounds that they were Irish.

His younger brother Thomas had one of the most extraordinary careers of that extraordinary time. He had left Wynford Eagle at the age of seventeen to go up to Oxford only three months before the Civil War broke out. Returning to join his brothers in Dorset he served throughout the war in which he was severely wounded. On demobilisation in 1647 he decided to take up the study of medicine, returned to Oxford and was created Bachelor of Medicine by the then chancellor, without having had any medical training or experience whatever, or indeed having taken any other degree. Next year he was made a Fellow of All Souls and the year after Senior Bursar. In 1655, having successfully petitioned Cromwell himself for a large sum of money in respect of his own and his family's expenditures and services, he resigned his Fellowship, returned to be married at Wynford Eagle, and then set up as a London doctor. In 1659 he obtained permission from the Council of State to leave the country in order to study at the famous medical faculty of the University of Montpellier. Not only was he a very successful practitioner, he established a European reputation on his publications, largely descriptive and entirely pragmatic that explicitly eschewed all theories and explanations. Slowly he won the approval of the (by now restored) Royal College of Physicians who granted him a Doctor's degree. Although the friend and correspondent of Robert Boyle and John Locke, he was oddly never elected a Fellow of the Royal Society, though he, if any man, personified its cardinal principle of taking nothing for granted and insisting on physical demonstration. One of his pupils was Sir Hans Sloane and he is linked to the scion of yet another distinguished son of Dorset by the marriage of his niece to the father of Sir James Thornhill, the painter and MP for Melcombe Regis. Sydenham left £30 to assist his professional education. From Wynford Eagle to Sloane Square or the Painted Hall at Greenwich may not look an obvious transition, but history, like the roads of West Dorset, has some unexpected turnings.

Since we have landed up in Wynford Eagle we may as well turn left along the pretty winding valley that leads to Maiden Newton, a curiously charmless little town for so lovely a part of Dorset, and there take the other road back to Eggardon. If there is no hurry, turn left down the dead-end road to Toller Fratrum (West Dorset villages are partial to genitive plurals in their nomenclature), a place of a remoteness one would have thought impossible so close to the main road. The church which stands on the edge of the farmyard has a twelfth-century carving of Mary Magdalene washing the feet of Christ with her tears. Everything except this detail has been destroyed which gives the motif an intensity that might perhaps have been lost had the work survived entire.

Back to the main road and then next left to Toller Porcorum, which, without being in any way remarkable, manages to suggest the world of Tom Jones and Squire Western. A mile or so out of the village a sharp left turn takes us up a very beautiful hill back to the crossroads at Eggardon. That leaves only one road untried, and it is the most exciting of the lot. Marked with a well-justified disclaimer of its status in the hierarchy of highways, it starts off boldly, rashly even, along the outer rampart of the fort. Should you meet a car coming in the opposite direction both diplomacy and driving skill will be needed. Off to the right is the last far from negligible remnant of the once great Powerstock Forest. A sharp dip with woods crowding the pebble-strewn road brings you to a farm from which no other house is visible. One begins to wonder whether the road has any serious intention of keeping going. But another twist brings another farm in sight and behind it the buildings of Powerstock railway station, on the branch line, only closed in 1972, from Maiden Newton to Bridport. For remoteness, beauty and impracticability it might have served as the inspiration for the comic artist Emmett. Once again the road swerves into a wooded gorge, to emerge suddenly directly under the church and just by the thriving pub of Powerstock (The Three Horseshoes: it piques itself on its catering).

Powerstock is the opposite of Abbotsbury in that it is almost entirely a working village, not a Fort Knox of the Golden Oldies. It clings decoratively to the sides of a steep valley and its church has one of the noblest Norman chancel arches in Dorset.

Whichever way one turns from Powerstock pleasure lies in store. The beauty we enjoy is, as so often, the consequence of other people's deprivation. In 1794 the last Duke of Bolton died, leaving large estates of which one extended over a great deal of West Dorset. The division of his lands between the two daughters who inherited was sufficiently ambiguous to offer footholds and handholds for the lawyers to keep a case going for the next seventy years, with the result that no money could be spent on improvements and developments. This has contributed substantially – there are other causes: the poverty of the soil, the lack of communications – to the Rip Van Winkle effect of this landscape. Sometimes a chain of causes has contributed. The most famous recent example occurred a few miles from Powerstock where the extreme conservatism of a ninety-year-old farmer who refused to allow any sprays, fertilisers or other agricultural chemicals to be used on his land preserved the ecology of an earlier age. The sale of his farm and its probable transformation by the use of such things provoked an outcry. A public appeal, liberally supported by the Prince of Wales, raised enough money to buy a good part of it which is now maintained by the Dorset Trust for Nature Conservation. To open this to the public would defeat its object.

To open or not to open? The days when Elizabeth Bennett and her relations could bowl up to the front door of Pemberley and be shewn all over the house in the absence of its owner have long gone. The increasing sophistication of international art thievery imposes increasing burdens on the owners of beautiful houses containing beautiful things. It is sacrifice enough to convert one's house from time to time to a public gallery. Buf if one has got to go back to the early Middle Ages and fortify the place against assault, the bill for the electronics (and the insurance), to say nothing of personal anxiety, renders the arguments for staying shut powerful indeed. Very few of the great houses in Dorset are regularly open.

There are several near Powerstock, some of which open their gardens or grounds. It is very much gentry country, as opposed to the neighbouring Marshwood Vale where Hutchins, the great historian of Dorset discussed in the final chapter of this book, writing in the second half of the eighteenth century, roundly states that few gentry have ever lived. In his day the roads in the Vale were passable only in the driest part of a dry summer so that ordinary social life was impossible. They are still slow going and never run straight.

But to return to Powerstock, or rather to turn away from it. Taking the road out to the north-east leaving the church on your right hand you drive through spectacularly lovely country, wild and little cultivated. At Mount Pleasant where five roads meet there are views in all directions and no house nearby. Yet just over the hill out of sight lies a house that is one of the sights of the country – Mapperton. Although the house itself is not open the gardens are, except at week-ends, every afternoon from March to October. Fine in themselves, they enjoy a natural setting of breath-taking beauty. In addition, they enable the visitor to see the house and its exquisite seventeenth-century stable blocks, more like pavilions for dancing and feasting than mere accommodation for quadrupeds. Candida Lycett Green caught its quality in the article in her series 'Unwrecked England':

The country around Mapperton is like an English Tuscany – small hills stretching away into the distance – but green and wooded. Whether you approach Mapperton from Beaminster below or winding up and over from Evershot, its position at the head of a sudden and secret valley is a complete surprise. You approach the house with its outbuildings, like a small hamlet huddled round it, down a short straight drive which leads you to the west front. It is shaped in a U, one side of which is formed by a small church, and before it are two ravishing Restoration stable blocks

which continue the courtyard effect and lead your eye out over a ha-ha to
level fields.

It is the quality, supremely, of domesticity. Mapperton is
large, handsome, dignified, but without the chill of intimidat-
ing grandeur. The fact that the church is part of the house
(there is a door leading into it directly from one of the rooms as
though it were the chapel) is characteristic. Until this century
Mapperton was never sold or forfeit to the Crown but passed
by descent through three or four families, none of them
distinguished in the history of the nation. It is this retirement
from affairs that communicates itself so agreeably to the
visitor. Even the Civil War seems to have made mercifully little
impact on Mapperton. Its then owners, the Brodrepps were
moderately prominent Parliamentarians who, like so many of
the country gentry, thankfully welcomed the return of Charles
II in 1660. It is appropriate that the present owners are the
direct descendants of the first Earl of Sandwich, picked by
Cromwell to command a regiment in the New Model and then
to serve as General at Sea, who was yet one of the two principal
architects of the Restoration and one of its most distinguished
servants both as Admiral and Ambassador.

Only a mile or two below Mapperton lies Beaminster
(pronounced Bemminster), a small, charming, largely stone-
built town. Nothing much goes on there, but the serious
necessities of eating and drinking are well attended to. There is
a good grocer, a bakery whose aroma would stimulate the
most jaded appetite, two or three restaurants and hotels, with
a high reputation for their food. Beaminster is more private,
less zestful than Bridport. Its streets are narrow and curling,
opening out into a central square. Down a little hill lies the
church, a fine one, with a tower of the Somerset type with
elaborate external statuary. After Judge Jeffreys' Bloody
Assize the butchered limbs of his unhappy victims were
exposed on the tower. Monmouth's Rebellion recruited its ill-
armed, untrained forces from the peasantry of Somerset and

Dorset and it was these pathetic innocents who paid the price of this futile political vanity.

Half a mile or so to the south along the main road to Bridport is Parnham, one of the most notable manor houses in West Dorset, which is open all day on Wednesdays, Saturdays and Sundays in the tourist season. Its character is more assertive, less retiring, than that of Mapperton. Both are essentially Tudor houses, that have been remodelled in the intervening centuries. Parnham's setting, a well-wooded park just outside the town, has great charm. But its unique attraction is the furniture workshops of its present owner, John Makepeace, which have carried the fame of Parnham far beyond the borders of Dorset. In the Civil War it was owned by the Strodes, a leading Parliamentary family with estates in Somerset and Devon as well as Dorset.

Beaminster is close to the northern and western borders of the county so it will be convenient to sweep round the frontiers. To the west of the town lies the pretty village of Stoke Abbott in a valley on the road to nowhere. Its name, like so many in Dorset, reveals the landed wealth enjoyed by the monasteries, in this case the Abbey of Sherborne. Further to the west and slightly to the north is the more wakeful if less seductive village of Broadwindsor where a north–south road intersects one running east and west. It was here that the hunted Charles II took refuge in a room at the village inn after the fiasco at Charmouth in September 1651. Because of its position on what was then a main road it was full of troops on their way south to embark for an assault on the last Royalist stronghold of Jersey. Fortunately for the King everyone's attention was distracted by the accouchement – in the inn itself – of one of the women the soldiers had brought with them. The residents of Broadwindsor were determined not to be landed with the maintenance of this poor little citizen and the soldiers would be gone in the morning. Hence their excitement. Broadwindsor's only other claim to fame is that it had one of the most delightful of seventeenth-century authors for its rector. Thomas Fuller's *Worthies of England* and his *Church History* are written with a good humour and a lightness of touch that made him, as he himself recognised, a favourite with the publishers of his time and have found him readers in succeeding generations. A temperate Royalist he had many friends on the other side and had the courage to champion a peace policy when his own side was on top.

His neighbours to the west suffered for their Royalism. The squire of Burstock, an almost inaccessibly hidden village approached along a narrow lane with beautiful views of the Axe valley to the north, was heavily penalised for his zeal for the King. The Pinneys of Bettiscombe offer a rare example of drawing advantage from political adversity. Azariah Pinney was convicted of taking part in Monmouth's Rebellion and sentenced to be transported to the West Indies as a slave, a form of punishment introduced some thirty years earlier by Cromwell. However he seems to have obtained his liberty, no doubt by a discreet douceur, and set up as a merchant and planter on the island of Nevis. Prospering, he returned to England and the fortune he founded enabled the family to build the exquisite manor house which remained in their hands until very recently. It also provided the funds for Racedown, another handsome family house built nearby about a hundred years later. Neither is open to the public though Racedown can be seen clearly to the left of the road to Crewkerne, a mile or two out of Bettiscombe.

The next village, Marshwood, unexciting in itself gives its name to the Vale over which it looks. Its remoteness, though not so absolute as before the coming of macadamised roads, still makes itself felt. The water-retaining quality of its blue lias subsoil yields rich crops even in the driest of summers. The Vale of Plenty is the nickname given it by less fortunate farmers. It is dominated by the profiles of the hills that wall it in: Lamberts Castle, Pilsdon Pen and Lewesdon to the north and north-east, Stonebarrow and Hardown to the south. Pilsdon Pen, bare and somehow suggestive of Mr Gladstone in full flood reproving the iniquities of the age, is in fact the highest hill in Dorset, though Lewesdon with its generous skyline of trees and its noble proportions might seem higher. Fuller, in whose parish they were, notes that

> Sea-Men make the nearest Relation betwixt them, calling the one the Cow, the other the Calf; in which forms it seems they appear first to their fancies, being eminent Sea-marks to such as sail along these Coasts. And although there be many Hills interposing betwixt these and the Sea, which seem higher to a land Traveller, yet these surmount them all: so incompetent a Judge, and so untrue a Surveyor is an ordinary eye of the Altitude of such places.

The Vale is not a place in which to be in a hurry. The roads do, ultimately, lead somewhere but wherever it is you could have got there much quicker by staying outside it. Nor, as Hutchins pointed out, is it the place in which to look for the parks and manor houses of the gentry, though the fertility on which they originally depended is evident enough. The wealth of the landowner found its way elsewhere, except at the southern edge of the Vale where the magnificent church of Whitchurch Canonicorum suggests, like its name, the wealth of the medieval church, whose immortality provoked a lay reaction in the Statute of Mortmain, and no doubt contributed to the Reformation itself. 'Mortmain', the dead hand, might, unchecked, engross the whole land or be used as a tax-dodge to evade the fiscal burdens of land-holding under the feudal system. The Canons commemorated in the place-name were those of Salisbury. Besides the tithe of so productive a parish there was the valuable shrine of Saint Wite – latinised as Saint Candida, though she is said to have been a Saxon, martyred by the Vikings. Both her origins and her career are lost to history, as is the rise and development of her miraculous curative powers. But her shrine (a thirteenth-century stone chest with three oval openings still used for written ex votos and supplications to the saint) survives in the north transept together with her remains – surely an argument in itself of miraculous powers when the fury of the Reformers against exactly this sort of cult is considered. It is one of only three such shrines in the whole of England and is still sought by pilgrims.

The church in which she is honoured is very beautiful. The soaring curve of the chancel arch, springing from an unusually low point, takes the eye at once. And the carving of the arcade of the north aisle is of exquisite quality, sharp, clean, alive. The stylised design of the westernmost arches suggests the waves of the nearby but invisible sea. The maritime connexion is echoed in a carved stone panel of a medieval ship high up in the northern side (exterior) of the extremely handsome tower. It is reinforced by the fact that Sir George Summers, a seventeenth-century sea-captain credited with the discovery of the Bermudas, is buried in the church. The islands were then uninhabited, except by herds of wild pig, off which Summers dined not wisely but too well with, unfortunately, fatal effects. Presumably he held house or lands in Whitchurch as his body was brought back here for burial. He was a Weymouth man by birth.

Whitchurch is a village which still retains a good deal of its charms. The Five Bells is a pleasant pub which serves food every day. The Shave Cross Inn, reached by twisting roads and existing on its deserved reputation as it has no village behind it, is closed on Mondays. It is well and truly into the Vale whereas Whitchurch is on the margin.

V

Dorchester and its environs

Since we are already in the west let us approach the county town from that direction. The Bridport–Dorchester road runs at its western end, a mile or two out of Bridport, over very high downs with a compelling prospect of the sea. It is often very windy and there are warning notices about high-sided vehicles. It is often very cloudy as waves of thick mist roll in from the Channel. It is sometimes both. But assuming a clear day there are good views to the landward side, notably of the village of Askerswell, just off the road that leads towards Eggardon, laid out below you rather as if it were an illustration to an up-market textbook about life in the medieval village. In fact closer inspection would reveal that most of the buildings are comparatively modern.

To the right, the conformation of the hill allows little foreground. Such land as you can see is far below and several miles away. We have already traversed it in Chapter III. But just over the brow of the hill, out of sight from the road is Chilcombe, a deliciously sited church (in the farmyard which is all the village consists of) with beautiful views and interesting features. It contains a wooden carving with scenes of the Passion whose origin, date and provenance are disputed. Everyone agrees that it is not English and no one knows how it ended up in Chilcombe, though one picturesque version (Michael Pitt-Rivers in the Shell Guide, 1966) records the story that it was spoil from the Armada. Most other guides assign it to the seventeenth century and some assert an Italian origin. Mediterranean, either Spanish or Italian, it clearly looks. And since guessing is free and scholarship is sacred I would guess sixteenth- rather than seventeenth-century. Loot from the Armada would have been well earned by the sizeable contingent of Dorset ships and sailors. But was any Spanish vessel driven ashore on this coast? One very badly burnt prize was taken into Weymouth but she hardly seems a likely source. It is an agreeable puzzle.

If one has the time to negotiate the lanes along the north side of the Bride valley, instead of speeding along towards Dorchester on the excellent hill-top mainroad, the next village along is Litton Cheney, unspoilt, unaffected and charming. The Old Rectory was for long the home of the great engraver and typographer Reynolds Stone, whose beautiful letter-cutting can be seen locally in many church memorials, and indeed on that which crowns the Golden Cap, recording its acquisition for the nation and preserving the memory of the Chairman of the National Trust under whom this was achieved. Reynolds Stone celebrated his house and its approach in a series of woodcuts and of watercolours which are among the treasures of the Dorset County Museum. The church is, like the village, charming and simple. The post office used to have the reputation of selling the authentic Dorset cheese called Blue Vinny whose methods of production were hardly such as to commend themselves to the bureaucracy of Brussels.

Between the extremely pretty villages of Long Bredy and Little Bredy is the long, narrow, elegant house of Kingston Russell, not open to the public but just visible to the eye of faith down a long avenue. Closer inspection would reveal an eighteenth-century entrance front, the central block of the best Portland stone, the flanking wings, added in the early twentieth century, mortared stone blocks of inferior colour. The garden front is a ravishing seventeenth-century stretch of mullion and transom windows held together by a central door-case with simple scroll-work decoration. Only one room thick the house has a lightness and a delicacy, a chamber-music quality.

Astonishingly it, and not the vast opulent sprawl of Woburn

Abbey, is the true cradle of the greatest of all Whig dynasties, whose stars have risen from the political to the intellectual firmament. John Russell, first Earl of Bedford, the subject of one of Holbein's most wonderful portrait-drawings 'Russell Lord Privy Seal with one eie', sprang from this quiet retreat straight to the court of Henry VII and to a career of soldiering and diplomacy crowned by wealth beyond the dreams of avarice. There is a fairy-story quality about his rise in piquant contrast to the grim Stalinist world of purges and executions that, under Henry VIII, offered such glittering opportunities to those who were adroit enough to survive.

In 1506 Archduke Philip, Governor of the Netherlands was passing down channel with his wife, Joanna the Mad, on their way to Spain when stress of weather forced them to put in at Weymouth. Past days of seasickness and the continuation of threatening weather disinclined them for an immediate resumption of the voyage. What was to be done with them? They could not just be left on the quay at Weymouth. England's relations with Spain were delicate. The betrothal of Prince Arthur to the Infanta Catherine of Aragon had been terminated by Arthur's death. Negotiations for the substitution of his brother Henry were not yet in train. Sir Thomas Trenchard, the head of the most important local family, at once invited the royal couple to his house at Wolfeton, just outside Dorchester, and at the same time sent to London for instructions. Before these could arrive he found his hospitality embarrassed by his own and his guests' ignorance of any foreign language, and he remembered that his young kinsman and neighbour, John Russell, had been sent abroad precisely to acquire this skill. Russell arrived hotfoot. The Archduke was charmed and, when invited to Court, took him as his interpreter. When the time came for him to resume his journey he recommended him to Henry VII who made him a gentleman of his household. But it was with Henry VIII, who succeeded three years later, that Russell established a rapport that not only lasted but deepened. At first the companion of his pleasures he soon won a reputation for courage and skill in arms, both on the field of battle and in the splendid tournaments by which the King set such store. His languages too gave him an opening into diplomacy which, combined with his military talent, made him the perfect instrument of Henry's aggressive and ambitious foreign policy. Honours and places were showered on him. The Reformation unlocked the vast landed wealth of the Church. An heiress and widow almost as rich as he became his wife. They lie together in a splendid chapel near Chenies, the house she brought him in Buckinghamshire. Woburn was just part of the monastic pick-up. By the end of his life the foundations of the family grandeur were all in place.

And here, in the Bride Valley, long deserted by their distinguished descendants, only two or three miles apart, are Kingston Russell and Abbotsbury, the seed bed of the Dukes of Bedford and the Earls of Ilchester, both the equals of Trollope's Duke of Omnium as Whig grandees. Dorset is adept at distancing itself from place and power.

But we must resume the main road to Dorchester from which Chilcombe distracted us. Not always visible in their full abundance, but visible enough, are the earthworks and barrows that remind us that we are not only approaching Dorchester: we are approaching Maiden Castle.

The concentration of prehistoric monuments round this, the greatest and best-known Iron Age hill fort in Britain, is thick. And much of it antedates the Iron Age. The most recent scholarly survey, 'The Prehistoric Hinterland of Maiden Castle' by Andrew J. Lawson in the *Antiquaries Journal* for 1990, places the earliest construction yet discovered at about 3700 BC. The reader who requires a summary of the present state of knowledge and an introduction to the extensive literature of the subject will find it there. A visit to the Dorchester Museum is of course the most obvious and most rewarding preliminary step. As you speed along the largely unbuilt-up A35 you can reflect that you are passing through what was once the most densely populated area of England, long before London was born or thought of. What were they like, our lost, invisible ancestors? We really have not the slightest idea. Their religion, their manners, their literature, if any, even their language has left no identifiable trace. We can find out quite a lot about their diet and the sources of their household goods, but unless one is an obsessional economic historian this still leaves them the shadow of a shade. And yet, and yet . . . People who go cub-hunting in these parts on misty autumn mornings feel that there are presences other than those of the hunt (and the occasional saboteurs).

Maiden Castle itself is best approached by turning off the main Dorchester–Weymouth road just outside the town – the site is about a mile to the south-west. If you take the by-pass, turn towards Dorchester at the Weymouth roundabout. The turn to Maiden Castle will then be on your left as you begin to encounter the first ample residences that form Dorchester's rather ordinary southern boundary. The earthwork itself is so thoroughly described in so many easily accessible guides that no attempt to do so will be made here. Its effect is proportionate to the solitude of the observer. Henchard's tryst in *The Mayor of Casterbridge* makes the point.

Dorchester has surrendered entirely to its fictional identification. Even sober-sided institutions like the Banks almost call themselves the Casterbridge Branch. And of course it is the brand name of all locally marketed consumer goods. Until ten years ago, Dorchester was still recognisably an old-fashioned county town with long-established shops. But shopping malls and supermarkets, worse still the horrible pseudo-Bavarian toytown that now stretches down between the Weymouth road and the railway are draining the blood from its heart. No effort of imagination could picture Farfrae on a summer's evening looking in through the window of the handsome hotel (still externally almost unchanged) in which the corn-chandlers were having their annual binge. In the 1970s and early 1980s it was still just possible.

Nonetheless the town has still much to offer – except, in

summer, somewhere to park. The High Street is still beautiful though it is no longer the pleasure it was to wander off down the quiet streets that lie to the south. The two principal southern tributaries, South Street and Trinity Street remind one of once handsome women who have mistakenly enlisted the aid of cosmetic surgery. The parish church stands four-square and challenging at the centre of things, a well-bred, good-looking building. Its interior is by comparison with-drawn and reticent. The great monument to Denzil Holles, sprawling in Roman get-up and wearing a full-bottomed wig, is meanly and darkly set, squeezed in like a rush-hour passenger. There are two other earlier, and more successful, seventeenth-century monuments to people no one has heard of outside Dorset. One is to Sir John Williams of Herringston, that beautiful house just off the road to Weymouth, and the other to Matthew Chubb, a Jacobean prototype of the Mayor of Casterbridge, who had risen from humble origins to become the richest man in Dorchester, and even MP for the borough. Unlike Hardy's mayor he managed to hold on to his winnings and improved them by two rich marriages.

Chubb and Williams were friends and political allies in the fierce political conflicts that raged in Dorchester under the first two Stuarts. The story is brilliantly told in David Underdown's book *Fire from Heaven* (1992). Not since the Iron Age, or perhaps the Roman occupation, had Dorchester occupied so conspicuous a position in the life of the nation. This came about through the coincidence of an extraordinary man and an extraordinary event. The man was a Puritan intellectual of great administrative talent who became Rector of the two principal churches in 1605 and the event was the great fire of 1613 which destroyed about half the town in an afternoon. So great a calamity could not, in an age which saw the hand of God in even the most commonplace phenomena, be under-stood as anything but a manifestation of the divine displeasure with the inhabitants. The Rector, John White, famous for his skills in the pulpit, was well able to make the most of such an opportunity. But beyond his narrow Calvinism was a widely informed and creative intelligence. He set about building, as David Underdown shows, a mini-welfare state with alms-houses for the elderly, a hospice for poor children, food and fuel for the needy, even a rudimentary health service. All this was financed by the profits of the municipal brewhouse.

White was not content to limit his horizon to the spiritual and material needs of Dorchester. The people of God, as he would have termed them, were having a hard time of it in the second quarter of the seventeenth century. At home, Charles I and Archbishop Laud were on the warpath against Puritanism. On the continent, the Thirty Years War had opened with the disastrous defeat of the Calvinist champion, the Elector Palatine who had unwisely accepted the invitation of the Bohemian nobles to become their king. White's curate in Dorchester was a refugee from the Palatinate. Only in New England, where one of White's nephews was a prosperous Boston merchant, were the Puritans coming out on top. White, who had been a Fellow of New College at the same time as the able Puritan politician Lord Saye and Sele, was in contact with the national leaders of what was to become the Parliamentary opposition to the King. He was the driving force in founding a local company for the colonisation of Massachusetts which ultimately merged with the Massachusetts Bay Company itself. A number of Dorset men sailed with John Winthrop, and White himself considered emigration. All this made Dorchester famous for its bold, missionary Puritanism. When, at last, in 1640 Charles I was forced to call a Parliament Dorchester might be counted on to return two members who would make their mark in opposition to the Court.

The two were Denzil Holles and Denis Bond. Bond became an important member of the Committee that managed the affairs of the navy during the Civil War that followed. But Holles earned a place in history as one of the five members whom the King tried to arrest in one of the most dramatic scenes in the whole history of Parliament. The figure who now looks down on you hardly has the air of a revolutionary leader. Nor was he. Like so many of the men who went up to Westminster in the autumn of 1640 he wanted to change the policies the King was pursuing and the men through whom he was trying to enforce them. He fought for the Parliament when it came to fighting. But it was not because he wished to change the frame of government. On the contrary he was expelled from the House of Commons in 1648 because of his outspoken opposition to those who did. Long before the Restoration he had identified himself with the cause of the King who, when he returned to claim his inheritance, rewarded his loyalty with a peerage.

Dorchester's hour of glory however had passed with the war. As the Royalist historian Clarendon gleefully pointed out the town that had established a reputation for the boldest resistance to authority in the days of peace proved itself the most craven in time of war. White himself simply ran away and the town surrendered to a far from overwhelming Royalist force without firing a shot. The grand system of social relief fell to the ground and the brewhouse, which had provided the means, though not entirely abandoned as a source of charity never regained its position. Once again the danger of eminence had been eluded. Dorchester relapsed into obscurity until drawn once more to the nation's attention by the novels of Thomas Hardy.

Dorchester is rich in museums. The specialist ones, the Dinosaur Museum and the Military Museum, which occupies the proud castellated gatehouse of what was the headquarters of the County Regiment, define themselves. The County Museum in the High Street is interesting both for its contents and for its construction, which includes a light, airy exhibition gallery with slim elegant cast-iron pillars now seen to advantage in the recently restored original colour scheme. Also preserved is the interior and furniture of Thomas Hardy's study, removed from Max Gate, the rather ugly house he built himself on the eastern edge of the town. Recently Max Gate has itself been opened to the public (Sundays, Mondays and Wednesdays 2.00–5.00 p.m.). The management of the Museum is imaginative and lively. It is much the best place to see the extensive remains of the important Roman town, mosaics especially. Apart from the agreeable and unexpected West and South Walks which follow the line of the Roman city wall there is little surviving evidence above ground and nothing in the atmosphere that suggests a Roman town.

There is a lot of pleasant eighteenth and nineteenth century domestic and commercial architecture. The churches have either been restored or completely rebuilt, scouring the grime and sterilising the vitality of the Middle Ages. Seen from a distance, especially from the north and the east, the dominating and beautiful feature of the skyline is the tower of St George's, Fordington, originally a suburb of Dorchester but now merged in the town. A closer inspection disappoints except, and it is a notable exception, for the large and arresting Norman tympanum. To the west of the town the experimental estate of Poundbury, laid out by the Prince of Wales on Duchy of Cornwall land, is beginning to rise. By the time this book appears it should be possible to judge how far the objections to the proximity to Maiden Castle are justified. Dorchester is fortunate in having its own excellent guide written by Jo Draper of the County Museum.

Within the penumbra of the town lie the two tiny and exquisitely beautiful parishes to which William Barnes ministered, Whitcombe and Winterborne Came. Whitcombe, now in the safe and sensitive hands of the Redundant Churches Trust, sits invitingly by the side of the road to Wareham within its own curtain wall. The interior does not disappoint. There is a fine fifteenth-century wall painting of St Christopher; a waggon roof; great simplicity, and an openness and absence of clutter. Winterborne Came, lovingly restored and again in the care of the Redundant Churches, is not easily found, sheltering deferentially behind the trees of the drive leading up to the splendid Palladian front of Came House (privately owned and not open to the public). Its interior is richer: a fine screen and beautiful altar rails, late Elizabethan and Jacobean monuments. The road running across the Park gives you a perfect view of the house.

Circling round Dorchester in an easterly arc from these two charming south-easterly neighbours one would come next to the village of West Stafford, a notably pretty place with a particularly interesting church plumb in its middle forcing the road into a blind right-angled turn. The interior is largely seventeenth-century but there is a magnificent eighteenth-century monument which gracefully bends its head to avoid hitting the waggon roof. At the other end of the village is an agreeable pub with the pleasant name of The Wise Man.

Almost due east of Dorchester, at the end of what must have been a noble avenue of trees now intersected by the by-pass and diminished but not destroyed by the ravages of time, stands Kingston Maurward, now an agricultural college. The house was built in the reign of George I and unhappily re-faced with Portland stone in the reign of his great-grandson. Houses, like people, lose a great deal of their personality by being institutionalised but perhaps this one had lost quite a lot in its days of independence. Yet even now there is a certain resentful grandeur in its distant aspect.

Due north of Dorchester across the valley of the Frome is a beautiful stretch of farming country untouched by development. Continuing to describe our circle towards the west from which we originally came, we are surprised by one of the most romantic and exciting houses in the whole county, seemingly left to slumber for centuries though it is in fact close to the important main road to Yeovil and Sherborne. This is Wolfeton, whose glorious fat gatehouse towers seem to promise a castle rather than a fortified manor house. Although in private hands and still in process of restoration by its owner the house is open to the public on most afternoons during the summer. During its early and great days it was the seat of the Trenchards, a leading Dorset family on whom, as we have seen, devolved the obligation of entertaining shipwrecked royalty. There are legends, of the type John Aubrey loved, attached to Wolfeton, presaging the ruin and disaster that would result from the Civil War. As the Long Parliament met the sceptre dropped from the carving of the King in the great hall. On a less portentous note the sound, said to be sometimes heard, of a coach and horses being driven up the great staircase by a Trenchard of a rather later generation suggests a tradition of conviviality.

As so often with the original houses of old families the conveniences and comforts of the eighteenth century led to reduction in the ranks. The Trenchards abandoned the house to bailiffs and tenant farmers but a great deal of beauty, particularly in the woodwork now in the great hall and in the drawing room, has survived.

Unusual and interesting as the house is, Wolfeton preserves intact one feature unique in Britain: an original seventeenth-century riding house where the art of riding the great horse was learned. The riding house is not open to the public but can be seen from outside.

Wolfeton lies within the parish of Charminster and it is within that beautiful church that the tombs of the Trenchards occupy their own chapel in the south aisle. With its double aisle and magnificent Norman chancel arch the interior is even more effective than its outside view promises. The nineteenth-century chancel makes inspired use of a seventeenth-century east window. The alternation of Norman and perpendicular windows in the clerestory provides an unusual example of the marriage of these two styles so happily consummated in a number of English cathedrals.

The Trenchards were prominent Parliamentarians in the Civil War. Sir Thomas's name stands second only to that of Denzil Holles in the County Committee appointed to levy forces and raise money by local assessment. Perhaps fortunately for the family, Sir Thomas died three years before the Restoration. His descendants sailed happily on, sitting as members for various Dorset boroughs and even for the county in the Parliaments of Charles II and William and Mary. The last of them, who had been High Sheriff in 1778, died less than a decade before Queen Victoria succeeded to the throne. Charminster church is among their memorials. They built the handsome bell-tower, a fact commemorated by the ornamental initial 'T's to be seen both outside and in.

VI
East from Dorchester

Between the modern main road running east from Dorchester and the line of the Roman road that diverges from it at Stinsford, a mile or two out of the town, lies Hardy's birthplace at Higher Bockhampton. The cottage, now owned by the National Trust, is beautifully kept and may be visited by appointment. The garden is open every day in summer. The surroundings, unselfconsciously maintained but not prettified or commercialised, still call the world of the novels to mind.

Puddletown Woods through which the main road now cuts like a motorway are generous enough to deserve the name of Forest which they are given on the map. The village from which they take their name is rich in interest and beauty if you take a few paces from either of the busy roads that meet there. Coming from Dorchester, the A354 to Blandford and Salisbury turns sharply off to the left, but for the moment we will hold to the coast road towards Wimborne and Bournemouth. Even the main street is not entirely devoid of a certain gritty charm (the baker's shop has a great reputation). But if you turn off left, towards the church whose tower may be seen looking at you through its lorgnettes across the intervening roofs, you are translated from a world of jumbo coaches and articulated lorries full of alarming-sounding chemicals into the

blest Regions meek of joy and love.

Or so, for a moment or two, it feels. The church itself is one of the best in Dorset. There is something from every period and all, like the Church of England itself when it is not shrivelled by zealotry, agree in a harmony of spirit. The building is almost entirely medieval, mainly of the fourteenth and fifteenth centuries, though there is a fine Norman font. But the special attraction of the church is its distillation of the spirit of the age of George Herbert, who was parish priest at Bemerton, near Salisbury, when the box pews and the gallery were put in during the 1630s. Herbert's hymns

> Teach me, my God and King
> In all things Thee to see

and the famous paraphrase of the Psalm

> The God of Love my Shepherd is

achieve a crystalline clarity, a simplicity that everyone can understand and a depth that no one can plumb, that should assure them immortality after the strenuous contemporaneity, now so much in fashion, has gone the way of all flesh. To this age too belong the Black-letter texts now flaking from the walls.

In the gallery it is easy to imagine the village band of Hardy's novels. In fact his grandfather played there before he built the cottage at Bockhampton. Thomas himself led an unsuccessful fight to defend the building, which had miraculously escaped the zeal of Victorian restoration, from the remodelling of the chancel in 1911. There are some beautiful alabaster tombs with recumbent effigies to be found there as well as a much earlier figure of a knight and lady in the south transept. Altogether the church is rich in monuments of every description and date, brass panels, stone entablatures, some with inscriptions that reward the reading.

Outside the church one recognises again what a delightful place Puddletown is. Its name incidentally derives not as one might think from the imagination of Beatrix Potter but from the river Piddle or Puddle, also known as the Trent, which finds its way into Poole Harbour at Wareham. The square and the vicarage have dignity without assertiveness.

To the east of the vicarage is Ilsington House, open to the

public in the season, with large gardens from which it is best seen. Essentially a handsome William and Mary building, it was somewhat harshly remodelled in the nineteenth century, and that is the impression conveyed by the glimpse you get from the main road.

Puddletown's most famous house is half a mile further east along the main road. Athelhampton shows what Stock-broker's Tudor could be like when actually built by a Tudor stockbroker, or his equivalent. Sir William Martyn's tomb is in Puddletown church. He was Lord Mayor of London in 1493 by which time he had started to build Athelhampton, a work continued by his heirs in the next century. No expense was spared and the house has been notably well cared for since. Osbert Lancaster's Stockbroker came from a part of the home counties where half-timbering was the idiom. Athelhampton, like nearly all the great houses of Dorset, is built of stone. It has features made familiar by the colleges of Oxford and Cambridge, a great hall and screen (not the original, but brought as a replacement from a house in Devon of much the same date), a splendid oriel rising almost to the full height of the room and a magnificent timber-framed roof. Athelhampton has been liberally open to the public but a recent serious fire may have imposed some temporary restrictions. The contents rather than the house itself suffered worst.

Even more remarkable and much earlier than Athelhampton though neither so beautiful nor, till recently, so well looked after is Woodsford Castle a couple of miles to the south in the Frome valley. You need a map and some ingenuity to find it but even from the outside you realise that you are in the presence of something rare. A thatched castle seems a contradiction in terms but Woodsford is the largest thatched building in England. Built in the fourteenth century it had fallen into decay before the Civil War in which, unlike so many of its Dorset brethren, it played no part. But so substantial a piece of masonry could always be put to some use, in this case as a farmhouse which it remained until its recent acquisition by the

Landmark Trust, that brilliant creation of the brilliant Sir John Smith. It is now being restored and fitted up for letting to visitors who like staying in beautiful and unusual places.

A mile or two further along the valley is Moreton with its delicious Georgian Gothick Church. So light and fragile it looks, an ecclesiastical expression of the persona of Fanny Price in *Mansfield Park*, that one wonders that the whole thing was not blown away like thistledown by the German landmine dropped nearby in 1940. It blew out the windows of the apse and north aisle, severely damaging the structure, but giving the happy opportunity for Laurence Whistler to engrave the glass that replaced them, recording in a wealth of elegant decoration the state of the church as it was when bombed and after restoration. The parish rightly takes great pride in its flower festival when the church is a sea of colour. In the pew of the Frampton family, who paid for the building, is a monument in which, to borrow Sir Owen Morshead's description, 'the long text is sprinkled with wild flowers sedulously carved in relief. It was executed by Peter Matthias Van Gelder of Amsterdam in 1762.' T. E. Lawrence, whose memorial is in St Martin's, Wareham, is buried in the cemetery across the road.

Striking back northwards towards the main road, which we abandoned at a boring and tortuous stretch, we reach the pretty village of Affpuddle. The Church of St Laurence, set delectably right on the river, is rewarding as well as beautiful. The sixteenth-century woodwork is particularly charming but, like Puddletown if in a minor key, it combines a number of periods without diminishing its wholeness.

We rejoin the main road at Tolpuddle, a village best known as a place of pilgrimage for the Labour movement. The idiot brutality shewn to the poor by the Whig government of the 1830s for once recoiled on its own head. The transported labourers, convicted of having taken an oath to combine into a trade union, were brought back and compensated, enabling some of them to establish themselves in comfort and respectability. The Martyrs Inn which celebrates their memory has a somewhat hair-shirted look: perhaps within there are merry peasants roistering round the pin-tables. From the placards pleading for a by-pass it seems that the inhabitants, with some justice, regard themselves as martyrs to the A35.

The road on towards Bere Regis begins to be beautiful with long views over attractive country to either side. Bere itself has been rescued from the twentieth century by a well-placed by-pass to the north-east from which the little town looks inviting. Should you succumb, the church is one of the stars in Dorset's firmament. The nave roof with its riches of carving and colour is particularly splendid. An unusual feature is that the hammer beams which support it are in the form of life-size figures, probably the twelve apostles, who jut out at right-angles from the walls as though they were hang-gliding. This magnificence may be attributed to the charity of Cardinal Morton, Henry VII's trusted adviser and the architect of the marriage with Elizabeth of York that ended the Wars of the Roses. Morton was born either here or at Milborne St Andrew (see p. 99) and endowed a chantry where the souls of his parents and himself might be remembered. This chapel is at the east end of the north aisle: that of the Turberville family (the d'Urbervilles of Hardy's most famous novel) across the church in the south aisle. The church is altogether extremely handsome, its western tower particularly so.

At the foot of the Bere by-pass the road divides, that on the right turning across the heath country towards Wareham and Bournemouth. Directly beyond the roundabout at which the roads divide rises Woodbury Hill, the scene of the fair in *Far From the Madding Crowd*. Taking the left-hand road towards Wimborne which runs through agreeable if not exciting country the most interesting and attractive places are mostly to the left, just off the road: Winterborne Kingston and Winterborne Zelston are both pleasantly becalmed little Dorset villages, typical but unexciting. But Anderson Manor and the parish church of Winterborne Tomson are among the treasures of the county. Anderson Manor is not open to the public and barely visible from the road, but it is a remarkably unspoiled, light, elegant Jacobean house, built of brick with stone quoins and dressings. There is a fine colour plate of it in volume III part I of the RCHM Dorset series. It was built in 1622 for a member of the Tregonwell family, who was himself a recusant and suffered accordingly in the Civil War. The Tregonwells, though some managed a precarious neutrality, were strong Royalists. John Tregonwell of Milton Abbas headed the list of Dorset gentlemen whom Charles II intended to honour in his proposed Order of the Royal Oak which never got beyond the drawing board. Since the qualification was to have served, or made sacrifices for, the Crown during the Civil War it would have perpetuated the divisions that the Restoration was designed to heal.

If Anderson Manor must be taken on trust by visitors the nearby church of St Andrew at Winterborne Tomson welcomes them (the prefix Winterborne refers to streams which only make a seasonal appearance as opposed to rivers which are, or were, always there). Winterborne Tomson is unique or rare in several aspects. It is unique in being the only apsidal church in Dorset to have survived from the Middle Ages. It is a twelfth-century building with sixteenth-century windows and, rare sight, an unaltered interior of early eighteenth-century box pews. It owes its survival in the first place to benign neglect and in the second to the inspired use made of money raised by selling some of Hardy's correspondence, itself a stroke conceived by the Powys family who carried out the restoration in a spirit which the great man would have applauded. The crowning touch is the Reynolds Stone inscription recording this admirable achievement. Winterborne Tomson is one of Dorset's title deeds.

Returning once more to the main road we soon find ourselves passing a wall on the right hand which seems to go on for ever. Behind it rises a thick screen of trees. At last on the angle of the road appears a handsome arched gate with a fine stag standing on top of it. Clearly, we are passing a great family seat. Indeed we are, and passing it must satisfy our curiosity since the house and the very grand park are not open to the public. It is Charborough Park, a house built by Sir Walter Erle, a great man for the Parliament in the Civil War and one of the managers of the impeachment of the Earl of Strafford that preceded it. Erle's son died in his father's lifetime and the house and estate have frequently passed through the female line so that the family have accumulated an unusual number of surnames, now hyphenated into Plunkett- Ernle-Erle-Drax. Sir Walter's house was, as might be expected, burnt and looted by Royalist forces, but he retaliated by repairing it with materials taken from Corfe Castle after its surrender. At the Restoration, the Bankeses demanded their restitution, but settled for a good sum. Nonetheless, the ashes continued to smoulder and an inscription on one of the ice-houses in the park, recorded by Hutchins in his *History of Dorset*, claims that the Glorious Revolution of 1688 was planned there in 1686 by 'a set of patriotic gentlemen of this neighbourhood'.

Attending a garden-fête at Wareham in the 1920s, the Lady Drax of the day found herself abruptly addressed by a woman she did not know: 'I think it is time that we talked to each other again'. It was Mrs Bankes of Kingston Lacy, closing the chapter that had opened in the time of Charles I. The house contains wall paintings by Sir James Thornhill, a member of an old Dorset family whose estate, lost through the father's extravagance, the son bought back by his successful practice as a painter. It will be remembered that it was the Sydenhams of Wynford Eagle who had helped to give him a start in life. The most conspicuous feature of Charborough, visible from miles away though not from the road along which we are travelling, is the tower erected in the Park as a folly in 1790 and shortly afterwards struck by lightning. It was then rebuilt and, defiantly, raised even higher.

Opposite the park wall as you first sight it coming from the west is Almer, a tiny place consisting of a parish church of variegated date and a pleasant Elizabethan manor house seen across a paddock from the main road. A little west of the church is a handsome Georgian brick farmhouse.

Still speeding past the great wall of Charborough we pass another splendid gate, this time with a lion on top of it. When we eventually emerge into daylight and champaign the country is rather duller. If you turn left at the next crossroads you can skirt the village of Sturminster Marshall, which visually does not live up to the euphony of its name, and cross the Stour by the beautiful and little frequented White Mill Bridge. Turning right, you can follow a picturesque by-road which will take you into Wimborne behind Kingston Lacy through the pretty village of Pamphill. Of course this takes about three times as long as sticking to the main road but it must be owned that the main road lacks charm. Henbury House, a late Georgian building easily visible up its drive just after the roundabout on your right, looks as if it has a hard-luck story it wanted to tell you. (In fact it has.) Corfe Mullen is a stunted-looking village. The church tower is much too stout and strong for its height, suggesting an encounter with the guillotine. A seventeenth-century manor house, or what survives of it, stands forlornly in some damp fields, not at all at ease with the featureless modern buildings nearby.

Wimborne is surprisingly attractive, astonishingly so when one sees that the tides of Bournemouth suburbia are licking its outskirts. And as at Dorchester the pleasant old-fashioned specialist shops which gave character and vivacity to its centre are falling victim to the supermarkets. Already there has been a good deal of unsightly redevelopment and it seems only too likely that there will be more. Nonetheless there is still some handsome, well-proportioned eighteenth-century urban architecture to form a setting for the Minster as, on a grander scale, the Close does for Salisbury Cathedral.

The Minster is one of the principal historical monuments of Dorset. Indeed the RCHM report rates it as second only to Sherborne. Both were cradles of Saxon Christianity. Wimborne is dedicated to St Cuthburga, sister to Ine, King of the West Saxons, whose code of laws is the earliest in our history (c. 690–693). Cuthburga was abbess of Wimborne in 705 when St Aldhelm, Bishop of Sherborne, dated one of his letters from there. The exterior of the abbey with its cheerful rather raffish mixture of stones of very different colours and its marked evidence of Victorian restoration hardly suggests ancient pieties. The most immediately attractive feature is the strong, self-confident Western tower added in the fifteenth century.

But when you step inside it is another matter. There is still the same air of lightness, frivolity almost, but it flickers over solid, unmistakable antiquity. You cannot see any Saxon work but you can feel its presence behind the Norman arcades of the nave and the tall simplicity of the crossing. The chancel which rises half a storey higher reinforces with its splendid Early English ornament the impression of an unbroken continuity of solemn worship. It is a church that you do not come to the end of at a single visit. There is a very fine thirteenth-century fresco of the Crucifixion, marred by part of another painted over it a century later and by clumsy architectural intrusion. There are a number of beautiful and interesting tombs from the Middle Ages to the eighteenth century. There is a famous chained library. Most insistent of all is the note of continuity. The Minster has a large and active congregation.

East from Wimborne the landscape, natural and human, is the most depressing in the county, a flat, heathy emptiness sometimes mercifully concealed behind a thicket of silver birches. Nursery gardens seem to thrive in such places: one thinks of Woking and its environs. But if you turn north, roughly in the direction of Salisbury, things are much better.

The road has the advantage of taking you to the Horton Inn where the food and drink are very good. To the right lies the village of Horton with a most unusual little church dedicated to the Saxon Saint Wolfrida, largely of the eighteenth century. The tower and spire are thought to have been inspired by Vanbrugh (he was working nearby at Eastbury in the Tarrant Valley at the time). Much more conspicuous, though architecturally less interesting, is the mid-eighteenth century folly, Horton Tower. It was built by a fox hunter who could no longer ride to hounds, in order that he could watch them work.

Horton church contains the tomb of another veteran of the chase who died a century earlier at the age of ninety-nine. Henry Hastings was squire of Woodlands a mile or two to the north-east. His young neighbour, the 1st Earl of Shaftesbury, has left a brilliant sketch:

Mr Hastings, by his quality, being the son, brother, and uncle to the Earls of Huntingdon, and his way of living, had the first place among us. He was peradventure an original in our age, or rather the copy of our nobility in ancient days in hunting and not warlike times; he was low, very strong and very active, of a reddish flaxen hair, his clothes always green cloth, and never all worth when new five pounds. His house was perfectly of the old fashion, in the midst of a large park well stocked with deer, and near the house rabbits to serve his kitchen, many fish-ponds, and great store of wood and timber; a bowling green in it, long but narrow, full of high ridges, it being never levelled since it was ploughed; they used round sand bowls, and it had a banqueting-house like a stand, a large one built in a tree. He kept all manner of sport-hounds, that ran buck, fox, hare, otter, and badger, and hawks long and short winged; he had all sorts of nets for fishing: he had a walk in the New Forest and the manor of Christ Church. This last supplied him with red deer, sea and river fish; and indeed all his neighbours' grounds and royalties were free to him, who bestowed all his time in such sports, but what he borrowed to caress his neighbours' wives and daughters, there being not a woman in all his walks of the degree of a yeoman's wife or under, and under the age of forty, but it was extremely her fault if he were not intimately acquainted with her.

This made him very popular, always speaking kindly to the husband, brother or father, who was to boot very welcome to his house whenever he came. There he found beef pudding and small beer in great plenty, a house not so neatly kept as to shame him or his dirty shoes, the great hall strewed with marrow bones, full of hawks' perches, hounds, spaniels, and terriers, the upper sides of the hall hung with fox-skins of this and the last year's skinning, here and there a polecat intermixed, guns and keepers' and huntsmen's poles in abundance.

The parlour was a large long room, as properly furnished; on a great hearth paved with brick lay some terriers and the choicest hounds and spaniels; seldom but two of the great chairs had litters of young cats in them, which were not to be disturbed, he having always three or four attending him at dinner, and a little white round stick of fourteen inches long lying by his trencher, that he might defend such meat as he had no mind to part with to them. The windows, which were very large, served for places to lay his arrows, crossbows, stonebows, and other such like accoutrements; the corners of the room full of the best chose hunting and hawking poles; an oyster-table at the lower end, which was of constant use twice a day all the year round, for he never failed to eat oysters before dinner and supper through all seasons: the neighbouring town of Poole supplied him with them.

The upper part of this room had two small tables and a desk, on the one side of which was a church Bible, on the other the Book of Martyrs; on the tables were hawks' hoods, bells, and such like, two or three old green hats with their crowns thrust in so as to hold ten or a dozen eggs, which were of a pheasant kind of poultry he took much care of and fed himself; tables, dice, cards, and boxes were not wanting. In the hole of the desk were store of tobacco-pipes that had been used. On one side of this end of the room was the door of a closet, wherein stood the strong beer and the wine, which never came thence but in single glasses, that being the rule of the house exactly observed, for he never exceeded in drink or permitted it.

On the other side was a door into an old chapel not used for devotion; the pulpit, as the safest place, was never wanting of a cold chine of beef, pasty of venison, gammon of bacon, or great apple-pie, with thick crust extremely baked. His table cost him not much, though it was very good to eat at, his sports supplying all but beef and mutton, except Friday, when he had the best sea-fish as well as other fish he could get, and was the day that his neighbours of best quality most visited him. . . .

He was well natured, but soon angry, calling his servants bastard and cuckoldy knaves, in one of which he often spoke truth to his own knowledge, and sometimes in both, though of the same man. He lived to a hundred, never lost his eyesight, but always writ and read without spectacles, and got to horse without help. Until past fourscore he rode to the death of a stag as well as any.

We have seen Shaftesbury as a vigorous, indeed ruthless, partisan first of the Royalists and then of Parliament in the Civil War. At the time that he wrote this extraordinarily vivid recollection of his old neighbour he was at the height of a political career that is one of the most dazzling in English history. He had been in the highest office. He had laid the foundations of a party system and of a regular, declared policy of opposition to the Crown, hitherto considered as synonymous with treason. And here he is, painting with a sharp observation of detail that suggests the Dutch school of his day, a portrait and a domestic interior that tells us more about the Dorset of his young manhood than any passage of comparable length.

'Only connect,' wrote E. M. Forster. What a connexion the life of Henry Hastings makes. Born in 1551, as a small boy he would have been able to remember the restoration of Catholicism, the Mass in Latin, the world of late medieval religion brought back by Queen Mary. Where his own sympathies in these matters lay is clear enough from the only two books to be seen in his house, the Bible and *Foxe's Book of Martyrs*, that manifesto of militant Puritanism. The 'Church Bible' of which Shaftesbury speaks was probably the Great Bible of 1539, printed in black-letter Gothic type before the division into verses had been introduced. The Authorised Version, which is what is usually meant by 'the Bible', was not published till 1611 and would have been regarded by the sixty-year-old Hastings as an innovation. The whole reign of Queen Elizabeth, the rising of the Northern Earls, the Defeat of the Spanish Armada, the voyages of Drake and Hawkins, the plays of Shakespeare, would have been mere episodes in a lifetime that ran virtually from the Reformation to the Civil War. His strenuous dedication to field, and other, sports would have helped to keep his mind off these things. Puritanism in his day had not earned its strong sexual connotation. The habit of temperance in drink, conspicuous in so slovenly and disordered a style of life, marks off the Elizabethan from the Stuart age. Throughout the seventeenth century foreigners remarked on the drunkenness of Englishmen of the upper class and Clarendon even thought it the principal cause of the Royalists' losing the Civil War. But we must turn from Henry Hastings and his house at Woodlands (of which a somewhat dilapidated fragment survives) to the house and village of his famous neighbour at Wimborne St Giles.

VII
The Dorset Dukeries

Outside the pages of *Zuleika Dobson* Dorset has no Duke, though the Sackville family briefly enjoyed this title for a few decades of the eighteenth century. But the clutch of great houses in the north-east corner of the county, Wimborne St Giles, Cranborne, Edmondsham and Moor Crichel invites a collective term. Wimborne, still in the possession of the family, was apparently the focus of the first Earl's affections. Inheriting as a minor, he began life with fierce grudges against his Trustees who, in his view, abused their position to enrich themselves at the expense of the estate. It was a considerable inheritance. The fine range of almshouses adjoining the church look much as they did when they were built in 1624 and the stable block, built at the same time as a riding house, like that at Wolfeton, but later converted, is further evidence of family wealth. Of the house to which they were adjuncts nothing remains since the great house in which the future Earl took such pride began to rise on its site in 1651. He entertained the King there in the 1660s and when at last his political recklessness seemed likely to cost him dear he took effective measures to convey his property to members of his family, so that 'my house at St Giles' might escape, even if its creator did not.

His fame has been eclipsed by that of the Victorian 7th Earl, the philanthropist and Evangelical, promoter as a young man of the legislation protecting factory hands from exploitation before the Trade Union movement had got into its stride. Both were devoted to the place, added to the house, and are buried here, although the 7th Earl had been offered the honours of Westminster Abbey. It is only recently that the house they loved has ceased to preserve their archives and possessions as well as their posterity. Not open to the public, it is only hazily visible across the nettles and docks of the park.

The church which stands just outside the park is an extraordinary compound of spacious eighteenth-century enlightenment and the dramatic heightening of religious sensibility aimed at by Sir Ninian Comper, who was called in after a fire in 1908 and given a free hand. The result is vigorously and lucidly analysed by Pevsner in his excellent Dorset volume. The village is small, charming, discreet, islanded from the twentieth century.

Barely two miles away to the north-east, nudging the border with Hampshire, lies Cranborne, in setting and architecture one of the loveliest of Dorset houses and in its association with a great political dynasty no whit inferior to its Whig neighbour. Although the house is not open to the public the wonderful gardens that surround it often are, so that you can easily comprehend and enjoy its effect. The gardens are the creation of its châtelaines, so that besides taste and knowledge there is an organic quality – not in the sense that refers to the disdain of chemicals and fertilisers, but in the sense that both are part of a living whole. No doubt if Le Nôtre or Sir Joseph Paxton had been given the job they would have done it differently, but the gain, if gain there had been, would have been at the expense of a marriage that is of rare beauty. As Odysseus pointed out to Nausicaa, a happy marriage delights friends and vexes enemies but what it really is is known only to the two persons joined together.

Originally a royal hunting lodge from which the large area to the north takes its name of Cranborne Chase, the house was bought from Queen Elizabeth by the second of her great Cecil ministers, Robert, whom her successor created Earl of Salisbury and Viscount Cranborne. He transformed the house while keeping much of the original structure, a process which accounts for its individuality. Though there are abundant evidences of late Elizabethan or Jacobean style and technique the whole character of the building, its reticence, its solidity, somehow resists this categorisation. The twin brick lodges, set at an angle to the entrance court to which they lead, have a delicacy that will be found in other details of the design.

No evocation of the house could rival that of Lord David Cecil in his *Some Dorset Country Houses*. He spent much of his childhood there and ended his long life on its land. 'Cranborne's charm', he then wrote 'is to me as powerful as ever, though seen now in the unillusioned light of old age.' Among his glimpses of its history he records the slaughtering of an ox in the hall by Prince Maurice's men to show their contempt for the then Earl's lukewarmness towards the royal cause. Clarendon makes him the target of one of his most withering phrases. Coupling him with the Earl of Pembroke, he wrote that they 'had rather the King and his posterity should be destroyed than that Wilton should be taken from the one or Hatfield from the other; the preservation of both of which from any danger they both believed to be the highest point of prudence and politic circumspection'. From the early seventeenth century, Hatfield was the principal seat of the Earls of Salisbury. Indeed, in the eighteenth century they took no interest in Cranborne. The Civil War Earl, whom Clarendon so heartily despised, must at least be credited with the beautiful west wing built in 1647, between the first and second Civil Wars. No doubt he valued Cranborne for its original purpose since Clarendon also tells us 'He was a man of no words, except in hunting and hawking, in which he only knew how to behave himself.' Clarendon's judgements of people are apt to be coloured by his warmth of temper. The Earl, the first Englishman to have mentioned Palladio, may even have travelled abroad with Inigo Jones. At any rate he employed a good architect, Richard Ryder, who is known to have seen the work of Inigo Jones and his son-in-law John Webb at Wilton.

Cranborne is a pretty village. The church, standing next to

the manor, has signs of departed grandeur. It was once a Benedictine priory, but had dwindled to insignificance long before the Reformation.

A mile to the south is Edmondsham, a noble Elizabethan house built on an unencumbered site a few years before Robert Cecil set about remodelling Cranborne. It was built for the Husseys but passed from their possession almost at once though they continued to supply parsons and squires to the county for several generations. They took the Parliamentary side in the Civil War. The house is sometimes open to the public; but the nineteenth-century alterations to the interior have perhaps diminished its historical and aesthetic interest. The wings, added in the eighteenth century, have been much admired for architectural good manners. There is an excellent photograph in volume V of the RCHM.

The last of this quartet, Crichel House, is still the centre of a large family estate. Those who live nearby have every reason for gratitude for the broad, beautifully maintained rides through the woods and across the fields that are open to walkers and horsemen. Crichel itself is sometimes opened or made available for meetings or charitable enterprises. The house is about a mile north of Witchampton. The RCHM report sums it up as a remarkably handsome example of a late eighteenth-century country seat which incorporates at its centre a more modest house built about the middle of the century. The man responsible for its extension was the fox-hunting maniac who built Horton Tower. He inherited the house in 1765 and most of the work was done in the 1770s.

Crichel has had to wait until the second half of the twentieth century before securing its niche in national history. 'Crichel Down' was for a decade or so a battle honour in the long war waged against the tyranny of bureaucracy. Part of the estate had been requisitioned by the Air Ministry for use as a bombing range. When it was no longer needed the Air Force turned it over to the Ministry of Agriculture. The original owners, wishing to repurchase, found that the Crown Land commissioners had sold it to someone else without informing them of this intention. A public inquiry was demanded and, thanks to the energy and spirit of its promoters, reluctantly conceded. The report severely criticised the arbitrary and disingenuous behaviour of the civil servants chiefly involved. The then Minister of Agriculture, though in no way responsible for, or even informed of, the action taken by his subordinates, resigned. Such principles of transparent honour deserve to be remembered, as does the defence of the rights of the subject which elicited them.

Crichel's other claim to fame centres on the handsome house in the nearby village of Long Crichel where a quartet of distinguished aesthetes and writers that included Raymond Mortimer and Edward Sackville-West spent their week-ends *in villeggiatura* in the decades that followed the war.

But enough of country houses and their inhabitants. What about the surrounding countryside? Just after the Horton Inn, on the left of the road as you go towards Cranborne is a striking example of the mutability of things – an abandoned site within an earlier abandoned site. Knowlton Church is a substantial medieval ruin, the village it served long since vanished. The church was still used up to the Civil Wars and then left derelict until about 1730 when it was resuscitated and struggled on till the roof fell in about the middle of the century. The henge within which it stands is Neolithic and there are traces of considerable Bronze Age settlements round about. Its proximity to a busy road conveys something of the effect of Belshazzar's feast.

West of Knowlton lie the three Gussages. Gussage All Saints has an elegant, spacious fourteenth-century church with an ugly nineteenth-century roof and a hideous East window. It is commended in Sir Owen Morshead's enchanting *Dorset Churches* where he points out that it shares with Tarrant Hinton the rare survival of an Easter Sepulchre, in which the Sacrament was kept and a watch set from Good Friday till Easter morning. The village is pretty, as is its neighbour,

Gussage St Michael. The last of them, Gussage St Andrew, reached by crossing the main road at Cashmoor (where there is a good pub) is the most independent: just a handsome farmhouse standing by itself on the shoulder of a hill with the little church above it; some much damaged wall paintings; and an atmosphere of regular worship that is surprising in a place that seems to have no discernible resident population.

Above the Gussages, to the south of the main road towards Salisbury, the landscape of Wyke Down is rich in Roman and prehistoric features. Ackling Dyke, the Roman road from Badbury and Dorchester to Old Sarum, is especially well preserved and at this point it cuts the Dorset cursus, a long prehistoric earthwork whose date and purpose are unknown. The Ordnance Survey is dotted with tumuli and barrows.

Vanished almost as completely is the most ambitious of all the great houses of this part of the country, the enormous mansion of Eastbury, just outside Tarrant Gunville. The present Eastbury House is simply part of one stable wing of Vanbrugh's design, the grandeur of which is only suggested by the gate piers on the public road. It was vast and, to judge from the paintings, somehow bogus. This judgement may take its colour from the personality of its only occupant-proprietor, George Bubb Dodington, a sham grandee who bluffed his way into a literary and political eminence culminating in a peerage. He has even won a place in the original *Oxford Book of English Verse*:

> Strive thy little bark to steer
> With the tide, but near the shore

sums up his public principles in a fair sample of his poetic talent. The territorial title that he chose, 'Melcombe', was perhaps an unexpectedly candid acknowledgement of the apothecary's shop in Weymouth said to have been kept by his father but more probably refers to his own Parliamentary control of that borough. At any rate he kept high state at Eastbury. He entertained Voltaire there and had Thornhill, who had painted a ceiling for him, returned to Parliament for Melcombe Regis, one of his pocket boroughs. Eastbury was never lived in after his death and his heir, despairing of a tenant, had it blown up after hardly half a century's existence.

Between Eastbury and the Gussages lies a happier survival from the eighteenth century, Chettle, just off the A354 and regularly opened to the public. It was built by Thomas Archer for the Chafyns, prominent Royalists, one of whom married a daughter of Colonel Penruddock, executed for heading a Royalist rising against Cromwell in 1655. Chettle is a delight. The double staircase in the hall sets a tone of exhilaration maintained by the light and space of the whole, a quality enhanced by the notable absence of clutter. The same character is evident in the beautiful and well-maintained garden, a naturalness and lack of fuss that sets off the house to perfection. Admirers of the architect can find his smirking, self-satisfied monument just across the Hampshire boundary at the attractive little eighteenth-century cruciform church that nestles under the shadow of another of his houses, Hale Park.

Chettle is set in a splendid park with a charming small village nearby. While cruising about this part of Cranborne Chase you may chance upon an old signpost on which the village of Sixpenny Handley is abbreviated, in terms of predecimalised coinage, to '6d Handley'. Do not be seduced into a deviation. It is not worth it. On the other hand the village of Ashmore, two or three miles in the opposite direction on the extreme northern border of the county, is enchanting. High up on the chalk downs of Cranborne Chase, it centres on a generous pond, a remarkable feature at the crown of a range of hills and obviously the work of man not nature. Claims are indeed made for its Roman origin. There is an unselfconscious winningness about this place. One can only wonder that it has escaped commercial development or the mischievous attentions of some government department. Let me write no more about it in case I excite such impure appetites.

But we have now done with the great houses that cluster round the Chase, still a fine stretch of country with handsome woods against which Uccello-esque scenes might be imagined, and we will turn to the other beauties of East Dorset.

VIII
East Dorset

From the western end of Cranborne Chase the Tarrant valley lies directly southward. Its villages reverently prefix their names with 'Tarrant', the broad Dorset pronunciation of 'Torrent', a description now scarcely applicable to the delicate stream, long enfeebled by the draughts swallowed by the water boards supplying the conurbation of Bournemouth.

Gunville, the northernmost, has been mentioned *en passant* as the parish to which Eastbury belonged. It is itself a place of considerable charm and has the special reticence that is characteristic of the Tarrant valley. Partly this is the effect of the scenery, generally narrow and steep and well wooded, and partly because it runs north and south while the main roads run east and west. The next village, Hinton, just holds itself in enough to escape the A354 from Blandford to Salisbury. The church contains an Easter Sepulchre of unusual beauty: it is Renaissance work of the 1530s, executed on the very eve of the Reformation 'which' as Sir Owen Morshead succinctly expresses it 'put an end to Easter Sepulchres'. The communion rails of Charles II's time come from Pembroke College, Cambridge, the patron of the living. How many colleges nowadays would think of the parishes in their gift when throwing out unwanted possessions with the philistine profligacy characteristic of such corporations?

A mile or two across the main road, Launceston, the next village, is hardly more than a sharp right-angled turn with a house or two. Monkton, barely half a mile off, is still a substantial place with a good pub and an attractive church, added to and patched up through the centuries. There is

78

nothing arresting and nothing out of place. As you go on down the valley, the hill crowds you to the left while on the right the river flows through a broad landscape rising gently to Monkton Down, behind which the army maintains the large base of Blandford Camp. Another couple of right angles bring us across the river to Rawston, now simply a large and prosperous farm in whose yard, invisible from the road, is a little church, beautifully kept but not in regular parochial use. Half a mile further on, to the left of the road and back on the east bank of the Tarrant, is Rushton, small and secluded with a charming if over-restored cruciform church. The lintel of the south door by which you enter is carved with a childlike, vigorous representation of the Lamb of God that suggests a prize-winner from one of the heavier classes at Smithfield.

Above the village is the site of Tarrant Rushton airfield, now restored to the growing of crops, from which so many exits and entrances were made in the 1940s by French resistance members and those who worked with them. The contrast between the tranquillity of this setting and the dark and terrifying world of underground warfare against the Nazis could hardly have been more striking.

At Keyneston the Tarrant slides under the Blandford-Wimborne road on to which we will, for a brief excursion, turn to the left in the direction of Wimborne. As you come up the hill you find yourself in the most spectacular avenue in Dorset, Badbury Avenue, which leads for a couple of miles past Badbury Rings to the home park of Kingston Lacy. Take care. The straightness of its course and the beauty of its beeches too often lull the motorist or excite the motor-cyclist into a careless euphoria. There are steep folds in the landscape which conceal oncoming traffic. Nasty accidents, in spite of the abundant warnings and double-white lines, are not uncommon. The generous verges are an invitation to the walker and the horseman.

Badbury Rings must detain all but the most famished culture-vulture, intent on the artistic riches of Kingston Lacy only a mile and a half away. Its great steep concentric ramparts command the landscape for miles around. An Iron Age fort, it was certainly occupied by the Romans, since two of the roads they built cross just to the south of it, one from Dorchester to Old Sarum, the other from Bath to Poole Harbour. More romantically but much less certainly, it may have been the Mons Badonis, the hill of Badon, where Arthur won his great victory over the invading Saxons, winning a reprieve for Romano-British civilisation against the lager louts who now seem, but let us hope only seem, to be having the last word.

The wood just to the north-east, on the bridleway leading to Witchampton is said to be haunted. People sensitive to such perceptions hear the noise of a large body of infantry on the march. Horses often shy or show signs of fear going through, but of course this may be caused by the effects of light or wind. Badbury itself before it was tidied up a few years ago was a gratifyingly sinister place on a winter afternoon, crowned with tall, unkempt woodland. Catherine Morland, fresh from her reading of Gothic novels, would have shuddered with delight. It is good to know that the excess of preservationism that cut down the trees and massacred the orchids has been tempered by a chaste and sensible replanting. The careless rapture may have gone but at least the taint of the municipal park is on the wane. Badbury is a favourite site for point-to-points. At least three hunts come here on successive Saturdays in spring. It is a wonderful setting and you can follow the race right the way round the course.

Returning to the Avenue and heading for Kingston Lacy, do not miss at the end of the Avenue on the left-hand side the elegant medieval house (not open to the public) now called Lodge Farm. Both the RCHM and John Newman describe it as a cottage, which would surely have struck a villein or a cottar as the understatement of a lifetime.

Turning into Kingston Lacy you are issued with a numbered ticket, much as one used to be at bus stops in Paris to avoid the unGallic denial of individuality implied by queueing. This will

Tomb of John Lewiston (d. 1584) in Sherborne Abbey. *Peter Burton/Harland Walshaw*

Thomas Fuller, Rector of Broadwindsor and author of *The Worthies of England*. *Fotomas Index*

Robert Gooden as he was in life. Monument in Over Compton Church. *National Monuments Record/RCHME Crown Copyright*

Chideock Castle: the final stages before demolition. *By permission of the British Library*

Thomas Hardy's cottage at Higher Bockhampton. *Peter Burton/ Harland Walshaw*

View towards the Hardy Monument – Nelson's Flag Captain, not
the writer. *Peter Burton/Harland Walshaw*

St George Reforne, Isle of Portland. *Peter Burton/Harland Walshaw*

A local stonemason's view of death and eternity: a tomb in the churchyard of St George Reforne. *Peter Burton/Harland Walshaw*

Portland Bill seen across Chesil Bank from hills above
Abbotsbury. *Peter Burton/Harland Walshaw*

Portland Bill in a rough sea. *Peter Burton/Harland Walshaw*

Mapperton: the house, with parish church on right. *Peter Burton/ Harland Walshaw*

Lyme Regis: the harbour, looking towards Golden Cap. *Peter Burton/Harland Walshaw*

admit you in your turn to the parties of thirty or so who are admitted at every half-hour to make the circuit of the house. Anyhow, it gives you time to make a preliminary appraisal of the house and its agreeable outbuildings.

As built by Sir Roger Pratt in the early 1660s it must have been one of the most beautiful country houses in Dorset. Pratt cannot compare with Inigo Jones for originality or for versatility or artistic talent, but if all the houses he had built could be seen as they were when he finished them he might be remembered as one of the most distinguished architects of the brilliant generation that succeeded Inigo. His one till recently surviving house, Coleshill in Berkshire, which was burnt down in 1950, displayed his imaginative handling of the great chimneys which were not required in the climate for which Palladio had designed his villas. There is still a faint echo of this at Kingston Lacy, but it is an echo drowned by Barry's assertive rehandling of the roof and grandiose expansion of the structure. It now looks less like a late seventeenth-century country house and more like one of the better clubs in Pall Mall.

Inside, the house is full of treasures. It will be remembered that the Bankes family had been the leading Royalists in this part of the county and that their seat, Corfe Castle, had been doughtily defended. Its slighting by the victorious Parliamentarians no doubt prompted the young heir, Ralph Bankes, to build Kingston Lacy, a house in which he could display much better than at Corfe his already considerable collection of pictures. A boy of twelve when the Civil War broke out, he had, like so many of the children of prominent Royalists, travelled abroad during the Interregnum. He was back in England by 1656 when he was admitted a member of Grays Inn where he made the first catalogue of his purchases. These included several of Charles I's pictures which, unlike those sold abroad and now in the Louvre or the Prado, had to be surrendered at the Restoration in 1660. Both patron and friend of Sir Peter Lely, he commissioned some of his most beautiful portraits and bought pictures through the artist's agency. This was the foundation of the collection so generously bequeathed, together with the estates of Kingston Lacy and Corfe Castle, to the National Trust three centuries later.

The other connoisseur who enriched the collection with an array of masterpieces was Byron's friend, William Bankes. The poet seems to have conceded him an admiring primacy in licentiousness. The nature of his tastes obliged him to live abroad, which enabled him the better to acquire the works of art which he continued to send back to Kingston Lacy. The Carrara marble staircase which he bought in Italy was an important element in the redesigning of the house undertaken by Barry.

The gardens at Kingston Lacy with their great cedars, some of which suffered in the gale of 1988, offer the most attractive view of the house. Behind them, towards the river, lies the wonderfully untouched village of Pamphill. The village green is delicious enough in itself but it is bordered by buildings of great charm and distinction. The Manor House and Gillingham's School and Almshouses silently reprove the grossness of the electricity pylons that deface and intrude – one of the worst instances of architectural bad manners in the county. Despite their stridency, the place remains its own private, retiring self.

Still on the Kingston Lacy estate and in the parish of Pamphill, though off to the left of the Wimborne-Cranborne road, is the notably handsome High Hall, not open to the public. John Newman's description of it in the *Buildings of England* emphasises its kinship to Kingston Lacy as originally conceived by Pratt.

But we must, to complete our excursion down the Tarrant Valley, retrace our course along Badbury Avenue and turn left through Keyneston where at the extreme western end of the village, beyond the church, there is a delectable walk beside the Tarrant itself to the last of the villages that bear its name, Tarrant Crawford.

Tarrant Crawford, or Tarrant Abbey as it is sometimes called on maps, is even smaller than Tarrant Rawston. There is simply one large house, not even a farm with cottages for the labourers, which probably incorporates some of the masonry from the outbuildings of the abbey that once occupied its site. For all its forgotten, withdrawn air it has its place in English history for it was here that Richard Poore, bishop successively of Chichester, Salisbury and Durham was born, and here in 1237 that he came back to die. Salisbury Cathedral was founded and built by him. Earlier in his career he had been Dean of the original cathedral at Old Sarum on the outskirts of the present city. Has any Dorset man left a more magnificent monument? No doubt it was in his honour that the church of Tarrant Crawford was so elaborately frescoed. The paintings though elegant and identifiable iconographically are faint. The church is still used once a month in summer for a joint service of the Tarrant parishes.

A few hundred yards downstream the Tarrant empties itself into the Stour at what is now called Spetisbury though the handsome medieval bridge by which one crosses is still called Crawford Bridge on the map, and the prehistoric earthwork on the far side of the Stour allows you the choice of Spetisbury Rings or Crawford Castle. We will in any case turn up the bank of the Stour towards Blandford.

Spetisbury is straggling and unattractive. But it is all but contiguous to Charlton Marshall, where there is a very handsome early eighteenth-century church with its original fittings, the work of the famous family of Blandford architects and craftsmen, the Bastards. The squalid vandalism of our age may render it necessary to obtain the key from Spetisbury rectory.

After passing through Blandford St Mary, an agreeable village that has survived years of being on a main road until relief arrived in the shape of the Blandford by-pass, you face the handsome gateway and magnificent woods of Bryanston. Bryanston shares with Stowe the brilliantly successful transition

– one would have thought it an impossible feat – from a great country house to a great public school. Both establishments, founded between the two world wars, from the first prided themselves on a libertarian style of life appropriate to the Whig aristocrats into whose inheritance they had entered. Stowe, the seat of the Temple family, still reflects in its house and grounds the grandeur of the eighteenth-century Whig supremacy. Bryanston, built by Norman Shaw for the second Viscount Portman in the eighteen-nineties, expresses the same note of self-confidence and enormous wealth but in a different idiom. The house, though invisible from the road, can be seen from miles away, standing with the strength and independence of a fortress. You can catch such a view of it where the road from Wimborne descends towards the roundabout on the Blandford by-pass.

The Portmans were staunch Royalists in the Civil War and ultra-Tory in the Parliaments of Charles II. In James's brief reign Sir William Portman showed his loyalist zeal in the energy of the measures he took against Monmouth, whom he personally hunted down and captured. Three years later, however, the wind had changed. He marched at the head of a large personal following to welcome William at Exeter in 1688. Thereafter the Portmans were Whigs, and in the nineteenth century, Liberals.

They were also great fox-hunters and their name is still honoured in that of Dorset's smartest hunt. But the legendary figures in this important department of county activity come from just the other side of the river. Peter Beckford, whose *Thoughts on Hunting* is known to most of us only through the reverence paid to it by that gloriously irreverent figure Mr Jorrocks, lived at the notably beautiful house of Stepleton Iwerne round which the Blandford–Shaftesbury road kow-tows in a series of right-angles. The rides he cut in the woods above for the training of hounds according to his system are still preserved. He fired his godson, Squire Farquharson of Langton Long, just over the Stour, with the same passion.

Farquharson is credited with a long famous run, some thirty miles, that ended with a death in an inn yard in Dorchester. Farquharson's name is preserved on the pub in Pimperne, at the heart of the Portman country.

Bryanston and Portman are familiar to Londoners as the names of squares on the estates which supported these splendours. The village of Bryanston is a pleasant little dependency of the great house. It is agreeable country for walking. The great woods border the road leading to the beautiful Winterborne valley. But we must cross the Stour to enjoy Blandford, one of the loveliest towns in Dorset.

Blandford, for all the ease and elegance of its appearance, has suffered in life's battles. Its Royalist sympathies exposed it to revengeful plunder by Parliamentary forces in the early summer of 1644 and the King's army returning from its victory at Lostwithiel a month or so later no doubt behaved with its usual vandalism and destructiveness. Early in October, Blandford was chosen by the Royalist command as the base from which Portland was to be relieved. The King's regiment of Horse Guards quartered at the village of Durweston while the Court lay in Bryanston. After the relief of Portland the war moved away. But in the following year the collapse of the Royalist position in the north and the midlands brought it back. The south-west was the King's last hope. Thither he had sent his heir to rally his quarrelsome and demoralised supporters. Naturally the Parliament, scenting final victory, were after them, so that once again Dorset was the field of conflict and its inhabitants the milch-cows of two opposing armies. It was this state of affairs that produced the Clubmen: and Blandford and the villages round it were prominent in the movement. Fairfax and his Lieutenant-General, Oliver Cromwell, were as conciliatory as they could be, but resolute and open in their refusal to tolerate any military force but their own. The Clubmen were divided: many of their leaders were crypto-Royalists who hoped to enlist the passionate and widespread war-weariness on their side. On the other hand much of the lawlessness and bullying that had goaded people into the movement was Royalist-inflicted. A large number of Clubmen made their peace with Fairfax and his officers. Two thousand or more who remained obdurate made their stand on Hod Hill, a few miles from Blandford in the parish of Child Okeford, and fired on the party who invited them to lay down their arms. The brisk action that put them to flight was the last that this part of Dorset saw of the fighting. But it had seen quite enough.

One of the most surprising features of this ancient market town is the absence of medieval buildings, silencing even the usual glib patter of the brown road signs that are generally met on the outskirts of anywhere with any pretensions to architectural beauty or historical interest. The explanation is simple: Fire. Camden in his *Britannia* (1586) records that the town 'having been by an accident burnt down in the last age save one, was rebuilt with great advantage, in point of beauty and number of inhabitants'. In consequence the corporation prescribed severe regulations to prevent a similar disaster. But without success. In 1731 the whole of the town centre was burnt to the ground. As on the previous occasion the consequence was fortunate. The Bastard family were not only at the height of their powers but also well placed in the civic hierarchy. The result was the building, over about thirty years, of one of the most exquisite Georgian small towns in England. Pevsner and Newman's entry in the Penguin *Buildings of England* does full justice to the whole and to the parts, so that only the sketchiest impression need be given here.

Dominating the town both from its interior, and from the distant prospect you get whizzing down the by-pass, are two buildings. The church, of St Peter and St Paul, built of green stone with Portland facings, rears its western tower over the tile roofs – thatch, which had contributed so signally to the 1731 conflagration, was forbidden thereafter. On slightly higher ground to the north stands a large brick house which looks as if it had escaped from a Rembrandt drawing – huge broad eaves, massive chimneys. It, together with the alms-houses in Salisbury Street built in 1682, is one of the few buildings that antedate the fire.

Salisbury Street contains a notable pork butcher where, besides the full range of porcine delicacies, local pâtés and local cheese are both excellent. Blandford still retains its true character as a market town. In spite of supermarkets there are still good shops in the market place. The bookshop in particular is much to be commended. And there are plenty of good pubs. The Crown Hotel by the bridge is large and comfortable and there is a French restaurant at the northern end of the town with a high reputation. Like Bridport, Blandford has great charm. It is always a pleasure to walk about it.

Apart from the Bastards, Blandford has not produced any distinguished sons. John Aubrey was at the grammar school as a small boy and remembered to the end of his life the severity of the punishment, but he had no other connexion with the place. The great Duke of Marlborough took the name of the town for the seat of his Marquisate which has since remained the courtesy title of successive eldest sons, but the Churchills for all their Dorset origins have had no particular affiliation with the town.

Since mention has been made of Stepleton and Hod Hill we may as well round off this chapter by taking the road towards Shaftesbury. It runs up the valley of the all-but invisible River Iwerne, which gives its name to two of the villages, Iwerne Courtney and Iwerne Minster.

Iwerne Courtney, most out of character for so open and trustworthy a place, has an alias: 'or Shroton'. The double-barrel is the original. 'Shroton' is thought to be a contraction of 'Sheriffstun' because, at the time of the Domesday survey, the village was the home of Baldwin the Sheriff. It is a pretty village whose church of St Mary contains an enormously elaborate monument put up in Cromwell's time. No puritan simplicity there.

Iwerne Minster is duller. Clayesmore School seems to have made it all neater and more regular than it would have been if left to itself. The church has interesting features, including that rarity in Dorset, a medieval spire.

We have been led on to these two villages because they bear the name of the river whose course the road follows. The first village you come to on leaving Blandford is Stourpaine, where the Steam Fair was first held, usually in late August (now moved to a site between Tarrant Hinton and Pimperne on the A354). A pretty place. But only a mile on is Stepleton House, with its two flanking pavilions added in the middle of the eighteenth century. The house itself, though modified about the same time, dates from Charles II's time. Newman suggests a close relationship to Hanford House, now a school, a mile away to the left on the by-road to Child Okeford. Stepleton is a handsome ensemble but do not try to take it in while driving as the road twists fiendishly and there is a good deal of traffic.

The Victorian church at Sutton Waldron was much admired by John Betjeman and is well described by Jo Draper. Fontmell Magna is, as its name suggests, large and handsome. Compton Abbas and Melbury Abbas, just off the road to the right, are both charming little places. But, as the road plunges downhill in front of you, there towers the hill of Shaftesbury.

IX
Shaftesbury and the North

Who does not know the much-photographed view down Gold Hill, the cobbled street, the stepped houses leaning against each other to avoid sliding down the hill with a vista of the Blackmore Vale far below stretching away into the distance over their irregular roof-line? Any tourist authority, hard-pressed for an evocation of England's timeless rusticity, reaches for it with confidence and relief. It is an effective, arresting picture, not least because the right-hand side of it, across the street from the houses, shows the hill rising sheer out of sight, supported by buttresses like the wall of a medieval church.

And it brings out, dramatically, the essential truth stated in the place-name. 'Burh' means a fortified administrative centre. 'Saxon hill-town' say the brown road-signs. And how! Zig-zagging up the hill from Cann, the last hamlet on the Blandford road, the defensive strength of the position is obvious. It is also strategic. The main road westward from Salisbury, the A30, and the South-Western railway line from Waterloo to Exeter pass along the Nadder valley immediately below (though comparatively little of the track actually passes through Dorset territory, mostly keeping in Wiltshire or Somerset just north of the county boundary, this line is known to connoisseurs of railway scenery as one of the most beautiful in England). King Alfred, who combined practicality with elevation of mind to a degree all too rare in our rulers, founded a nunnery here as well as creating a burh to defend it. Where he led, others followed. The town became prosperous and important, particularly after the Nunnery, or Abbey as it had become, gazumped its rivals by securing the bones of Edward the Martyr. Shrines and relics were the path-finders of the tourist trade. As soon as the weather begins to be half-decent as Chaucer observed 'then longen folk to goon on pilgrimages.' Shaftesbury was not so easily accessible to the main centres of medieval population as Canterbury but it is hard to realise in the present rather cold, wind-swept town, more than a shade reminiscent of some douce Scottish township, that it was once a hive of activity, supporting, besides one of the largest and richest nunneries in the country, a dozen churches and chapels and boasting its own mint.

The dissolution of the monasteries and the iconoclasm of the Reformation obliterated all that. It is hard to think of a medieval town of comparable importance and wealth where so few external signs of the Middle Ages survive. Even the most modest Dorset village can generally put on a better show. But nothing except the frequent drifts of rain-sodden mist can rob the place of its marvellous views; and the riches of its past can, to an extent, be recovered in the Museum.

So conspicuous a stronghold was bound to suffer the depredations of the Civil War. The fluctuating fortunes of the war in the south-west exposed it to occupation by both sides. In 1644 it had the misfortune to be assigned to a regiment of the King's army on its westward march which was composed of Swedes, Germans and other mercenaries. In the following year it was an obvious centre of operations for the Clubmen. In this part of the county they were very much under the control of the Royalists. Early in August they assembled at Shaftesbury with the intention of relieving the Parliamentary siege of Sherborne Castle. Swift action by Fleetwood, Cromwell's future son-in-law, resulted in the surrender of fifty of the leaders, some of whom were Royalist clergy evicted from their livings, one of them a kinsman of Clarendon, the great Royalist propagandist and historian. Throughout the interregnum Shaftesbury remained a danger spot. As the Restoration approached a number of plots for seizing it for the

King were reported but fortunately for the inhabitants nothing came of them.

Apart from the southern road up which we have come, the Dorset hinterland of Shaftesbury is not nearly as attractive as the Wiltshire environs to the north and east. The little salient that pushes out beyond Gillingham, a town signally lacking in charm, has no striking features. To the south-west there are some pretty villages, Stour Provost and Marnhull among them. Marnhull's church tower stands magnificently. Unlike Stour Provost, which is a neat, compact little place, Marnhull seems to have been blown about by a storm wind. Assuming that the church marks the centre, you find bits of it lying about all over the place, including a very fine stone farmhouse and barn, probably dating from the late sixteenth or early seventeenth century, called Pope's Farm. A little way beyond it to the south-west you cross the Stour by King's Mill Bridge, a notably elegant structure with the old millhouse just above it on the eastern bank.

If pursued, this road will take you to Stalbridge, an uninviting, narrow hole with some beautiful features hidden away if you bother to look for them. Jo Draper's Dorset guide takes a much more sympathetic and better informed view of the town. But if you take the other road southward from Marnhull, you will reach Sturminster Newton, which is incomparably nicer.

On the way, you pass through the village of Hinton St Mary, now characterised by raw, aggressive-looking council houses, but once evidently the seat of some Romano-British grandee since one of the most beautiful mosaic pavements in England, now in the British Museum, was found here. Sturminster itself (Newton, with which it is joined, is in fact a separate village just across the Stour) is strongly seventeenth-century in character. Large, islanded buildings whose amplitude takes no account of the motor car, still less of the articulated lorry, remind one of the townscapes so lovingly and minutely recorded by Wenceslaus Hollar. Although some of the generous gables that smile serenely over the market place are decorated with ornamental woodwork of that period, the bulk of the domestic architecture is eighteenth-century or Victorian, sometimes, as in the case of shopfronts, applied to earlier structures. It is still the market town it has always been, though French restaurants come and go, and the shops and pubs are good. There is an excellent bakery and till a few years ago there was that rarity, a working saddler who could restitch and repair any kind of leatherwork.

Like Blandford, Sturminster suffered from a serious fire in the eighteenth century but it was not so annihilating. The church which stands apart from the centre on the banks of the Stour is uncompromisingly medieval in appearance and design, though in fact most of it is skilful and scholarly nineteenth-century extrapolation of a comparatively modest fourteenth-century original. Dorset's heart beats in Sturminster. William Barnes, who was born in the village of Bagber just outside, went to school here and started life as a clerk in a solicitor's office in the town. Sir Owen Morshead, the author of *Dorset Churches* and a great figure in the Dorset Historic Churches Trust to which all lovers of the county owe so much, lived here for the last quarter of his long and distinguished life.

Crossing the Stour by one of the best of Dorset's medieval bridges we come to Newton, once the site of a castle that commanded the river crossing and the Blandford-Sherborne road, but now simply a pretty village with a mill still working which you can go and see. Turning east you come almost at once to Fiddleford (see p. 105), one of the medieval treasures of the county. Turning off the main road to the south you soon approach the most thrilling scenery in this part of Dorset. Almost immediately the road divides and presents you with a delectable choice. Either road will ultimately, but not swiftly, take you to Dorchester. But if you are in a hurry to get there, stay on the main Sherborne road until you have passed the village of Lydlinch and find yourself in the unreformed, unenclosed Lydlinch Common where Tom Jones or Squire Western might recognise the England they knew. Turn left here, and after you have passed the handsome park of Stock Gaylard, with its generous and decorative herd of fallow deer usually in sight of the road, turn left again. It is a pleasant but unexciting road and the villages of King's Stag and Pulham have nothing much to commend them except the pub at King's Stag which is an excellent place to pause for refreshment.

But in a more leisurely style we were just leaving Newton and considering the alternatives. If you take the right fork you will, after you have passed the turn for Plumber Manor whose simple workmanlike name contrasts with its Lucullan reputation for comfort and gastronomy, enter on a list of Dorset place-names as seductive as any. Fifehead Neville, Hazelbury Bryan, Mappowder, Plush! How could one distil a headier evocation of an England without filling stations or supermarkets? And the places are not unworthy of their calling.

Fifehead Neville boasts a pack-horse bridge over the little river Divelish (the old spelling of the village of Dewlish with which it has no obvious connexion) and a church, largely remodelled in the eighteenth century, containing a monument to one of the most fiercely Royalist of the strongly Royalist Ryves family.

Hazelbury Bryan, like Marnhull, is a dispersed settlement. The fine fifteenth-century church can be run to earth in one of its constituent hamlets succinctly named Droop. But the most beautiful church on this road, and directly on it, is Mappowder. Elegant, well-proportioned perpendicular is seen to advantage in this small-scale building: so often one thinks of the style deriving so much of its effect from sheer height. There are earlier features: a twelfth-century font and a small effigy of a knight. From Mappowder the road begins to climb. Plush is just what its name would lead one to expect – encouraged, as one has been, by a signpost that couples it with the all but invisible hamlet of Folly. Prettily set among the hills, its pub, The Brace of Pheasants, is also a popular restaurant.

The other road from Newton – the left-hand fork – is even more rewarding. The country you go through is beautiful and beautifully empty – hardly a farm, still less a village till you come to the steep flank of the hill that turns into Bulbarrow. As you twist round its hairpin bends, you become aware of a very considerable Victorian establishment, with great stable blocks and model cottages for the estate workers clinging to the side of the hill below you. This is Woolland, where another famous artist, the sculptress Elizabeth Frink, spent the last twenty years of her life.

Emerging on Bulbarrow, you will want to stretch your legs. The views over the Blackmore Vale are glorious. And Bulbarrow itself is a generous, welcoming hill with plenty of room for walkers and riders, and magnificent woods. Whichever direction you choose to take, there are pleasures in store. Down below you, a mile or two north-east of Woolland, is Ibberton, a pretty village that also clings to the side of the hill. 'Cling' is indeed the word; the parish church nearly lost its grip and, beginning to fall down from its perch, was abandoned in the nineteenth century, luckily to be restored at the beginning of this. It is dedicated to St Eustace, one of the patron saints of hunting, appropriately in this part of the country which is seen to such advantage from the saddle.

But if you turn your back on the Blackmore Vale – hard to do from such a vantage point – you can make your way to a positive host of Anstys, all of them more or less beautiful, Pleck or Little Ansty, Higher Ansty, Ansty Cross and Lower Ansty. Just after Ansty Cross there is a well-known inn called The Fox in which the offices of easement are labelled 'Dogs' and 'Vixen'.

From The Fox it is but a step to Melcombe Bingham which offers you two contrasting pleasures. Either you can leave your car and take the track to the right that leads up past Higher Melcombe to the Dorset Gap, a famous point of vantage from which on a clear day you can survey the whole county from east to west. In any event it is a most agreeable walk. Or, even more excitingly, you can take the lane to the left and after a mile or so park outside the avenue that leads up to Bingham's Melcombe. Although the house is not open to the public there is a right of way to the charming and beautifully kept church which adjoins it.

The whole scene, avenue, house, church and enfolding hills, is breathtakingly beautiful. Dorset, that country policeman so unobtrusively effective in the arrest of time, can show no happier example of its peculiar gift. The Binghams, whose name is so repetitively coupled with that of the place, remained in uninterrupted possession of it for six centuries. The last of them only sold out in 1895. Although you cannot visit the house you can read a vivid description of it in David Cecil's *Some Dorset Houses*. The different gardens behind it, the bowling green laid out in Henry VIII's time, the great yew hedges, the medieval gatehouse, bring before our imagination the England of Shakespeare. It is, of course, an exclusively rural image of that England.

For all the tranquillity and remoteness of their home the Binghams were active in affairs. In the Civil War they were prominent Parliamentarians and the house was the head-quarters from which the local militia organised its attack on Corfe Castle. Earlier, in Elizabeth's time, Sir Richard Bingham had earned a great reputation for his courage and skill in fighting both on land and at sea, and a less enviable one for his ruthlessness as a Governor of Connaught. The extent and variety of his service contrasts with the dreaming countryside that bore him. He marched with Protector Somerset against the Scots in 1547, he fought with the Spaniards against the French at St Quentin, he took part in a naval expedition against the Hebridean islands at the time of Queen Mary, he served with the Venetians against the Turks under Don John of Austria, and he fought at Lepanto and the taking of Cyprus. In 1578 he was fighting for the Dutch against the Spaniards and, two years later, was Captain of the *Swiftsure* in a grimly successful naval expedition against a Spanish force that had landed in County Kerry in support of the Irish rebels, against whom he was later to do such execution. As Governor of Connaught he was no less ruthless against the shipwrecked survivors of the Armada in 1588. Two of his brothers supported him in his Irish exploits and from one of them the Earls of Lucan are descended.

The eighteenth century and perhaps prolonged exposure to the pacific influence of Dorset seems to have mellowed the family. One of them, a learned clergyman, was a staunch supporter of Hutchins in writing the great *History of Dorset* but the last flowering of their military talent earned a knighthood in the Peninsular War. The village that once clustered round the church had disappeared even by Hutchins's time and now there is only the silence and the tombs of the family in the light and airy church.

Spreading out the map – you will need a map to get anywhere from Bingham's Melcombe – you have the choice of retracing your steps to Ansty Cross and then taking the road eastward towards Hilton and Milton Abbas or carrying on to the south for a couple of miles and then turning west towards Cheselbourne and Piddletrenthide. Let us postpone the first choice to another chapter and opt for the second.

The road to Cheselbourne preserves the solitude and beauty to which this central upland part of the county has accustomed us. Cheselbourne itself straggles agreeably, not sluttishly, along its valley. The church of St Martin is handsome, at the opposite end of the village to the turn to Piddletrenthide. This is a notable road with fine views to the south and a great sense of space and light. You run up and down great hills with long stretches along the tops until at last you plunge down a steep hill shadowed by magnificent beeches into Piddletrenthide at a fairly blind crossroads.

Piddletrenthide, like Cheselbourne, dawdles along a valley at even lazier length. Sometimes you feel you are never going to get to the end of it. Its inhabitants must have felt this for there was originally a lavish provision of public houses at which one could pause to recruit one's strength and resolution. There are fewer than there were but it is still a comforting adequacy.

The little river along which this picturesque village lies is, of course, the Piddle which offers a more refined version of its name, the Trent. The 'Trent' of Piddletrenthide is not, as one might guess, a polite correction of the vulgar form but a contraction of 'triginta' signifying that in the Domesday survey the parish was rated at thirty hides – a measurement of land whose exact significance is uncertain. Entering the village from Cheselbourne, as you turn right you will see immediately on your left a handsome three-storey late eighteenth-century house, now divided into flats, but once the manor house that looked across the present road to its naturally well-landscaped park, of which the great beeches that shaded your descent from Cheselbourne formed the right-hand verge. The old village street runs behind the manor, about a hundred yards to the west parallel with the present one and unmetalled. Walking along it, you get a sense of the deep rurality that still happily persists. At the end of it you come to the very fine parish church of All Saints with its notable western tower dated 1487.

The church, most beautifully set, is at the extreme north end of the village. If you turn round and come back by the modern motor road you will pass Pear Tree Cottage, an unusually well-built and highly finished sixteenth-century example of a type of dwelling that rarely commanded such attention. Re-passing your point of entry you will come, among other charming early nineteenth-century buildings, to the village school whose gates are, extraordinarily enough, the ornamental iron gates of an early sixteenth-century tomb in Westminster Abbey, which the Dean and Chapter, with the light-hearted philistinism characteristic of such bodies, threw out in 1820. A patriotic native of Piddletrenthide, who had prospered as a jeweller and silversmith in London, bought them and presented them to the school. Perhaps our masters will privatise them.

On and on you wind down the Piddle valley without coming to the end of the village. In fact, it doesn't end but just changes its name to White Lackington, which in turn merges into the more concentrated village of Piddlehinton.

Piddlehinton, too, has a beautiful late medieval church (St Mary). That the living was a good one is clear from the handsome mid-eighteenth century Glebe Court, originally the rectory. It was part of the foundation endowment of Eton College and retirement to it was till recently one of the rewards for service to which an Eton master in holy orders might aspire. Its neighbour, Piddletrenthide, was part of William of Wykeham's endowment of Winchester.

After Piddlehinton a sharp right-angle turn brings you down to the crossing of the Piddle and the division of the road. If you go straight on you come over a ridge to one of the most attractive views of Dorchester, but if you turn left you pass close to, and get an appetising view of, Waterston Manor – not open to the public but brilliantly described by Newman in the Penguin guide. It is largely early seventeenth-century.

The road winds on down the Piddle valley, debouching on to the A354 Blandford road at Puddletown. In the next chapter we will take it. But we will conclude this one by swerving to the left into the secret undisturbed country that lies towards Bingham's Melcombe and glance at the village of Dewlish. The alternative form Divelish is doubtless original since it nestles in the valley of a stream called the Devil's Brook, though why so innocuous a rivulet should claim kinship with the author of all ill is not apparent. The village is set on a steep descending curve which emphasises the prominence of a fine early seventeenth-century house at its centre.

Outside the village and historically unconnected with it is Dewlish House, a large, genial-looking, Queen Anne house built by a city man who reinforced his social claims by displaying his arms in the pediment of the north front. The house is not open to the public.

X

Milton Abbas and its neighbourhood

The two villages on the Blandford road, Milborne St Andrew and Winterborne Whitechurch are both attractive. Milborne St Andrew contends with Bere Regis for the claim to have been the birthplace of Henry VII's great minister, Cardinal Morton. Very much a Dorset man, he went to school at the monastery at Cerne Abbas before going up to Balliol and a successful career as an ecclesiastical lawyer. This led naturally to a career in government but the Wars of the Roses made this a risky occupation and Morton, for all the swiftness of his footwork, had some narrow squeaks. But his nerve and skill paid off and he ended up as both Archbishop of Canterbury and Lord Chancellor as well as Cardinal. He was a great builder and a generous patron of learned men, perhaps a role model for the better known Wolsey in the next reign.

The church contains some fine tombs of later members of his family, who were great people here till the eighteenth century. It also has a remarkably fine Norman doorway. George Orwell's grandfather was rector here and rebuilt the parsonage.

In the main village street is a private house, doubtless once a pub, with a life-size white hart on top of its porch. The white hart in question played an important part in Dorset's history. Henry III had admired it on one of his hunting expeditions to the Blackmore Vale and had reserved it for the pleasures of a future chase. To his fury, the animal was killed and eaten by a mere Dorset gentleman. This is the kind of thing that monarchs won't stand for. He imposed in punishment a special tax on the whole neighbourhood to be paid in perpetuity and to be known as white hart silver. Even the good-natured Thomas Fuller as rector of Broadwindsor was grudgingly paying up in the 1630s: 'Myself hath paid a share for the sauce, who never tasted any of the meat; so that it seems King's Venison is sooner eaten than digested.' Winterborne Whitechurch is prettily set in its valley. There is a good pub and a very good shop conveniently set back from the main road where you can buy superior victuals if you are catering for yourself or picnicking. The church contains a painted pulpit said to have come from Milton Abbey, to which we can make our way either from Milborne or Whitechurch.

The Whitechurch approach to Milton Abbas is the more dramatic. You turn sharp left down a steep little hill and find yourself confronted by a village apparently from a very grand toy department which has, by a wave of the magic wand, been transformed to life size. The impression is not essentially misleading. It is a model village and it was built as the plaything of a plutocrat. Joseph Damer, first Lord Milton and subsequently created Earl of Dorchester, married the heiress of the last Duke of Dorset. He thus disposed of resources that enabled him to do anything he wanted. First of all he commissioned Sir William Chambers to build him a Gothick mansion adjoining the abbey and then he decided to get rid of the small market town that had grown up round the abbey over the centuries since its foundation by the Saxon King Athelstan. The landscape was re-shaped as though during the first week of the Creation, though even in late eighteenth-century England the powers of a landed proprietor stopped short of the divine and the process took rather longer. The burghers were booted out and re-housed in the village, complete with its church, built for that purpose. However unedifying the story of its origins, it must be admitted that the result is remarkably beautiful. Uniformity of design – except for the late seventeenth-century almshouse which was bodily removed from its old site – does produce a striking effect. And unlike other model villages one can think of, Nuneham

Courtenay in Oxfordshire for example, the close well-wooded valley in which it is set gives it a feeling of intimacy rather than of regimentation. It is certainly one of the sights of Dorset, and there is a pleasant pub at the head of the village from which to survey it.

But this is only a foretaste of pleasures to come. At the bottom, where the lake and its steeply wooded shores stretch away, take the right-hand road up the hill. A little way up the hill, at an acute angle, there is a track leading up through the trees to St Catherine's Chapel, a pilgrim shrine of simplicity and beauty, enhanced by its emptiness and solitude. It is a very short walk and well worth it.

Returning to the road a couple of hundred yards further on, a turn to the left takes you down to the abbey itself, now a public school, but with liberal accommodation for the parking of cars and the visiting of the splendid church and grounds. Naturally the house itself, occupied in the business of education, is not as a rule open to the public, except in the Easter and Summer holidays when it is open every day. Outside, the house hardly does justice to its breathtaking site, the beauty of its materials (the best Portland stone) and the reputation of its architect. Perhaps it is paying the penalty of too much money. It goes on too long, like a boring story or a straggling village. But there is a certain worthy, weary respectability about it. It does not jar.

Inside, it is both more interesting and more beautiful, incorporating as it does the original great hall of the abbey. The townsfolk whose successors were so summarily evicted in the eighteenth century have a claim on our gratitude for having bought the abbey church at the time of the Reformation for their own parochial use. The buildings and grounds were bought by the Tregonwells, a Cornish family who rose like so many through success in civil and ecclesiastical law – the all but essential requirement for diplomatic or administrative employment. Dorset seems to have suited them. They built, as we have seen, Anderson Manor and were strongly Royalist in the Civil War. It was a John Tregonwell who, in 1674, built the almshouse here already noticed. Was he the same John Tregonwell whose monument in the abbey tells us that he died in 1680 at the then great age of eighty-two? His long life was the more miraculous because at the age of five he had fallen from the abbey roof. His petticoats, billowing out, acted as a parachute. To the amazement and delight of his appalled nurse he at once got up and began to pick daisies.

The abbey church, in which both he and his ancestor old Sir John Tregonwell, who took the surrender from the last abbot in 1539, lie buried, is light and lovely. Considering the antiquity of its foundation and its evident wealth there must have been a Saxon and a Norman church of some stature. But there was a fire early in the fourteenth century and everything that we now see dates from the rebuilding that followed. Only the chancel and the transepts had been completed by the time of the Dissolution so that one enters the church directly under the crossing – and what an entry it is!

Both the transepts have magnificent windows: the south of a slightly earlier period with decorated tracery that flows and swims, the north more severely perpendicular. But any touch of severity is more than counterbalanced by the luxurious monument to the great plutocrat himself, raising his head with the support of his right arm to gaze upon the exquisitely recumbent figure of his heiress-wife who predeceased him. Their riches did not make for a happy family life. Their eldest son spent money like a maniac, and when his father refused to pay his debts shot himself. The tomb was designed by Robert Adam and the sculptor was Carlini.

But the church, redolent though it is of the comfortable circumstances of late medieval monasticism, raises thoughts and spirits above the unhappiness of having too much money. The tower which from the outside reminds one of Sherborne reminds one of it again by the elegance and accomplishment of its vaulting. The choir, or presbytery, is simpler. But the reredos and, in particular, the sedilia are decorative and graceful without being in any way opulent. There are a number of interesting features, including a very, very rare survival: an elaborate wooden pyx-case, which might at first sight be mistaken for a font cover. It hung from the roof and was used to house the pyx, the vessel in which the consecrated host was reserved.

The admirable example of conservation shewn by Sir John Tregonwell and the townsmen of Milton Abbas was followed by their neighbours in the extremely pretty village of Hilton, which you reach by continuing further along the road that you have been on. The route also affords some notable views looking back over the playing fields of the school towards the abbey and the house. Hilton church is beautiful in its own right; but its special feature is its north aisle which was brought along the road you have just come by, stone by stone. It is part of the cloister of the abbey. There are also some paintings, of no great merit, which once formed part of a screen there.

All around you is the magnificent landscape of the Milton Abbey estate: great hanging woods, steep combes, and paths and bridleways from which you can enjoy them. Not that the roads in these parts suffer from an excess of traffic; it is an enchanted part of Dorset.

If you had not taken the Milton Abbas road in Winterborne Whitechurch you could have gone north up the highly attractive Winterborne valley. Just half a mile or so outside the village on your left you get an excellent view of a handsome eighteenth-century gentleman's residence surveying you benignly from a comfortable height and distance. This is Whatcombe House, built in the middle of the century and enlarged at its end.

Winterborne Clenston, tiny but pretty, has a neat, delicate little church entirely rebuilt about 1840, before the high tide of Victorian ecclesiastical revivalism. It is the kind of thing Edmund and Fanny Bertram would have put up in their old age, assuming, as I think we are entitled to do, that Edmund would have refused preferment in favour of continuing his ministry in a small out-of-the-way country parish. Jo Draper's entry on it is notably good.

Winterborne Stickland is a great contrast: a large, long village, some of it very ugly and some rather beautiful. The church, like so many Dorset churches, has interesting features from almost every period. Continuity is one of the holds that the past has on our imagination, nowhere more strongly exerted than in Dorset. The elegant Latinity of a memorial to his wife put up by a clergyman, almost certainly a dispossessed Royalist, in 1653 is encouraging evidence of how tenacious our forebears have been of what they thought valuable and important. Newman's entry on this village is most informative.

As one goes on up the valley one reaches its most beautiful part, where the great range to which Bulbarrow belongs rises to your left. Turnworth is on the opposite slope to Ibberton and even smaller. Its church was largely rebuilt in late Victorian times and Hardy, in his years as a prentice architect, had a hand in it. He long retained an affection for the place and used Turnworth House, now demolished, as part of the background for *The Woodlanders*. As at Bulbarrow there is a car park at the top of the hill where the National Trust owns a magnificent stretch of country, ideal for walking, riding and picnics.

Reluctantly descending the hill in the direction of Sturminster you are rewarded by the village of Okeford Fitzpaine, conspicuous for the handsome brick houses, some of them timber-framed and thatched, instead of the stone and cob, the characteristic materials of the county. Crossing the main road at New Cross Gate – incongruous echo of a focal point in the communications of South-East London – you reach the wonderfully becalmed village of Hammoon. The road goes no further, and the sense of the receding tide of history – a different, more romantic aspect than its continuity – is palpable in a majestic farmhouse, evidently once a much grander establishment. This is the manor house of the long extinct Mohun family, from whom the village derives its name. The de Mohuns came over with the Conqueror to become one of the great families of England. The place puts one in mind of the elegiac *obiter dictum* of Lord Chief Justice Crewe trying the De Vere peerage case in the time of Charles I:

> ... I suppose there is no man that hath any apprehension of gentry or nobleness, but his affection stands to the continuance of a house so illustrious and would take hold of a twig or a twine thread to uphold it. And yet time hath his revolutions; there must be a period and an end to all temporal things – *finis rerum* – an end of names and dignities, and whatsoever is terrene – and why not of DE VERE? For where is BOHUN? Where is MOWBRAY? Where is MORTIMER? Nay which is more, and most of all, where is PLANTAGENET? They are entombed in the urns and sepulchres of mortality.

Returning towards Sturminster, a turning to the right brings you to the much-admired manor house of Fiddleford, an extraordinary survival of the high Middle Ages. It is open to the public, indeed overwhelmingly so since no one lives there. The carved woodwork of the roof is exceptionally fine. You can walk there from Hammoon but there is no road. Down on the Stour there is a handsome sixteenth-century mill with an inscription addressed to the miller, dated 1566, that breathes the no-nonsense rectitude of Elizabethan England. The meadows of the river with their view across towards Sturminster have great charm.

XI
Sherborne and its approaches

Between Sturminster and Sherborne lie the Caundles —
Bishop's Caundle which the road goes through, and Purse
Caundle and Stourton Caundle to the north. Bishop's Caundle
has a strong, tall, fifteenth-century western tower that you can
admire from close to without leaving your car.

Purse and Stourton Caundle are both charming, Purse
particularly so by virtue of its remarkably well-preserved
fifteenth-century manor house, one of the best in the county,
which is occasionally open on summer afternoons. Even if it is
not there is a wonderfully graceful oriel window giving on to
the street which is one of the best architectural details in
Dorset. Wake Court, which as its name suggests was once the
seat of the Wake family, is no longer a country mansion but
produces an agreeable white wine something in the style of
that made in Baden.

If you have turned off to Purse Caundle your nearest way to
Sherborne is to push on for half a mile and then turn left on to
the A30. After crossing a salient of Somerset which contains
the large village of Milborne Port you re-enter Dorset at the
small village of Oborne just where the South-Western line
from Waterloo to Exeter sweeps down towards Sherborne.
Near the line is a tiny sixteenth-century ecclesiastical building,
obviously no longer in use, which looks as if it might have been
the mortuary chapel of some family too grand to be buried in a
mere churchyard. It is in fact all that remains of the original
parish church. A completely new one was built at the other end
of the village in the mid-nineteenth century.

But you will not want to be bothered with Oborne while to

your left opens the truly spectacular view of Sherborne Castle with its lake, its woods and its park. What you see riding the ridge is the massive and still almost opulent ruin of a great medieval castle. Closer inspection will show you an elaborate formation of ornamental chimneys standing apart from the original castle, peering at you rather nervously across the intervening landscape like a covey of pheasants. This is the tip of the Elizabethan house built by Sir Walter Ralegh and bought after his fall by James I's ambassador in Madrid, Sir John Digby, later created Earl of Bristol. The Elizabethan house, originally called Sherborne Lodge to distinguish it from the castle proper, was built on a slightly lower ridge a few hundred yards to the south. In the middle of the eighteenth century, Capability Brown, in one of his most inspired remodellings of landscape, filled the depression between them with water to form the lake, which you cannot see from the road, but which, on closer inspection, fills the heart with pleasure.

Both Castles – the old and the new – are regularly open to the public. The old, under the auspices of English Heritage, *pourvu que ça dure*, all the year round; the new, still in the possession of the Digby family, from Easter to September on three or four afternoons a week. Both amply repay a visit.

The old castle was built by Roger, Bishop of Salisbury in Henry I's time when bishops were very much involved with the administration of government and the maintenance of that rare and valuable commodity, the King's Peace. Twelfth-century England, like Europe in general, was by our standards wild and violent. Roger was one of Henry's Justiciars, that is one delegated with royal powers when the King was not there to exert them in person. On Henry's death in 1135 the fat of anarchy was truly in the fire. The nineteen long winters when, as it was said, Christ and his saints slept, ended with an exhausted truce and the accession of Henry II, one of the most original and effective rulers in our history. Roger, in spite of doing his best to keep in with the usurping Stephen, was soon forced to surrender Sherborne, along with his other castles, to the King. The castle thus became part of the royal demesne and was not restored to the bishops of Salisbury for another couple of centuries. They held on to it, and the large estates which supported it, until Queen Elizabeth, always disposed to reward her servants with the wealth of the church, forced the then bishop to grant it to Sir Walter Ralegh in the last decade of her reign.

Ralegh did not enjoy this splendid acquisition for long. At first he thought of living in the castle and began to make the keep and the gatehouse habitable. But a vast medieval fortified palace rarely visited by its owner is not easily converted to a desirable residence. He therefore set about building the lodge. The accession of James I, intent on an Anglo-Spanish entente, put Ralegh in the Tower and led, after an interval, to the granting of the estate to Sir John Digby and his elevation to the Earldom of Bristol. However, once again Spanish politics shaped Sherborne's destinies. The failure and humiliation of the Spanish marriage project led to Bristol's recall and disgrace. Since he was not welcome at Whitehall, he came down to Sherborne and, building on Ralegh's foundations, completed the lodge, henceforward to be known as Sherborne Castle.

It was here that he brought up his brilliant and politically disastrous son, George, who flashed across the skies of the seventeenth century, astonishing and entrancing an exalted audience both English and European. His knowledge of languages, acquired during his father's embassy, his wide reading, his captivating charm and physical grace brought him a premature prominence that he was ready to do anything to maintain. He certainly made his mark in the society of pre-Civil War Dorset as his contemporary the future Earl of Shaftesbury, who never liked him, admits in his memoirs. This glittering figure was returned as one of Dorset's two county members to both the Parliaments that met in 1640. At once he ranged himself with the leading critics of the Court and was one of those chosen to manage the impeachment of Strafford. But when the impeachment failed and the House decided to proceed by Act of Attainder, the Parliamentary version of lynch law, Digby championed the rights of the man whom he had been trying to bring to justice and was one of that small but heroic band – only fifty-three members in all – who voted against the Attainder.

At once he was welcomed by the King and Queen – especially the Queen over whom he easily established a special ascendancy – and called up into the House of Lords during his father's lifetime. But unhappily the scrupulous concern for Parliamentary justice that had occasioned the change does not seem to have survived it. Digby, as his friend Clarendon makes clear, was the instigator of the disastrous attempt to arrest the five members – two of whom, as we have seen, had strong Dorset connexions – which made the Civil War inevitable. When it came Sherborne Castle, like Corfe, became a stronghold of Royalism. Digby himself was out of the country – his outraged former friends in the Commons had impeached him of High Treason – and the small Royalist force which occupied the castle was commanded by the elderly and bookish Marquess of Hertford. Early in September 1642 – the Royal Standard had been raised at Nottingham only a fortnight earlier – a large Parliamentary force commanded by the Earl of Bedford arrived in Sherborne to besiege the castle. These were early days and the ordinary decencies of life were still respected. Lady Digby was Bedford's sister. He accordingly sent her a letter warning her to clear out before things got too hot. She immediately mounted her horse and rode to her brother's quarters to tell him that if he persisted in his intention he would find his sister's bones in the ruins.

The story suggests that both were agreed on the probable result of an action between two such disproportionate forces. But the small Royalist garrison contained some first-class officers, including Hopton, perhaps after Prince Rupert the best fighting leader on the King's side. They repeatedly took the initiative, beating up the besieger's quarters at night and making the best use of their slender resources of artillery during the day. The disconcerted Parliamentary forces drew off towards Yeovil with their tails between their legs. Boldness had paid off.

Sherborne Castle, like Basing House, was to remain a Royalist strongpoint dominating the road to the south-west until the very last stages of the war. In the end it was stormed by Fairfax after a sixteen day siege in August 1645 and orders were at once given for the slighting of so formidable a fortification. Its then commander, Sir Lewis Dyve, was sent prisoner to Westminster where, on his refusal to kneel at the bar of the House of Commons, he was sent to the Tower. His wife, who was pregnant, was refused access to him and both she and their child died. Dyve however escaped from the Tower in 1648 and got away to France.

So much for the old castle. Its successor is more of a curiosity than a thing of beauty but its contents are very well worth seeing and some of the rooms are indeed beautiful. There are a number of fine pictures, including a portrait, described as being of the 1st Earl of Bristol, which is almost certainly of his son, George, whose colourful career as we have seen began from this house.

The park, the lake, the *tout ensemble* of the two castles constitute one of the sights of Dorset. But down the hill and across the railway line lie the town, the School, and the Abbey, all of them famous and beautiful. Common to all of them is the soft-toned yellow ochre stone quarried nearby. There is very little brick in the town but what there is fits the elegance of the eighteenth century that employed it. Together with the stucco of a few Regency buildings the harmony of style and material is most satisfying.

Both logically and aesthetically the Abbey comes first. Long ago, almost a thousand years, Sherborne *was* a cathedral town, of which it still retains the feel. But in 1075 the see that had been founded for St Aldhelm was moved to Salisbury –

and who could regret that? But the great church and the school that from the earliest times had flowered against its walls remained. Sherborne has claims to be the oldest school in England and may even boast King Alfred as an old boy. Winchester and Eton are six or seven centuries junior. But the Abbey is the root of everything, School and town, and to that we gratefully turn.

No one will quarrel with the RCHM's judgement that it is the single most important church in Dorset and the most beautiful. Like Milton Abbey its antiquity is concealed by the glories of its reconstruction, caused as there by a devastating fire. In Sherborne's case it was actually deliberate malice, not accident. Bad relations between the monastery and the townspeople led to this violence. Traces of the earlier church can be discovered. There is some Saxon work in the west wall and Pevsner detects some in the crossing whose soaring piers have the splendid simplicity of Norman architecture which provides so perfect a frame for the elaboration of perpendicular, here seen at its loveliest in the fan vaulting of the nave and the choir. The piers of the nave are draped in perpendicular vesture but their spacing suggests that the masonry at the heart of them is much earlier. Traces of the fire can still be discerned in the reddening and darkening of some of the stonework of the crossing.

There are beauties beside the supreme beauty which the perpendicular achieves at Sherborne – so much lovelier than St George's Windsor, with which it is more or less contemporary. There is nothing chilly about either the proportions or the materials: and the atmosphere of a long continuity of congregational worship has its effect. The south transept is dominated by a huge monument to the 3rd Earl of Bristol – the dim son of the glamorous figure whose career has already been touched on. Its splendour and the grandiloquence of its inscription bring home just what a nonentity he was. There are other tombs aplenty, among them the effigies of Sir John Horsey and his son gazing out of their military get-up with the vacuity of the landed classes at some public function which they hope will soon be over. Why were they left unvandalised when Parliament's troops triumphed? Could it be because a member of the family was himself an officer in Rainborough's regiment, killed at the siege in 1645? Beside them, and almost their contemporary, is the tomb of John Leweston and his wife under an even more graceful canopy. He was the last of a family still represented in the place-names of the county.

There are several tombs of medieval abbots and a coffin into which, somewhat ghoulishly, one can peer through a glass panel. But rich as it is in monuments it is the building itself that stays in the mind.

Its exterior, particularly to the south which is not obscured by the buildings of the school, much of them monastic in origin, is magnificent. Several Norman details, such as the arch and the porch by which one enters, are obvious to the least expert eye. Equipped with Pevsner's excellent account in the Penguin guide there is more to be discerned. And his whole account of the buildings of the town is so succinct and informative that no attempt will be made here to do more than wave a hand in the direction of the chief riches of the place. The fifteenth-century almshouse in Trendle St, just to the south-west of the abbey, is remarkably well preserved and still retains in its chapel a fine Rhenish triptych. The cloisters and other monastic features are incorporated in the school to the north of the church.

Moving away from the abbey, the secular buildings of the town are outstanding. Particularly notable is the monastic lavatorium, where the monks once washed, now moved from its original site to serve as a market cross and known as the Conduit. Cheap Street the fascinating north-south thorough-fare, is so called not from the prices in the shops (which are some of the best as well as the most handsome in Dorset) but because 'Cheap' was the Saxon word for market – as in Eastcheap, Cheapside, etc.

The geography of the school, or rather schools, is complicated.

Apart from the famous public school there is also a scarcely less well-known girls' school, Lord Digby's School, which possesses one of the most handsome of the town houses, with wall paintings by Thornhill. Instead of knocking down existing buildings and concentrating everything in an academic laager, a bolder and more sensitive policy of acquiring and converting property as it came on the market has been pursued. The schools and the town are thus part of each other.

Sherborne is almost as much of a county town as Dorchester. Its shops are better and there are just as many good places to eat and drink. It is the natural centre of a generally prosperous agricultural hinterland where hunting and shooting are an important part of life. But it is not sunk in chawbacon rurality. You will find – if you wish to – chiropractors and Tandoori restaurants. It has an unselfconscious sense of continuity, with its own Saturnalia, celebrated each year on the second or third Monday in October.

Had one approached the town along the main road from Sturminster, instead of turning off up to Purse Caundle, one would have come down a steep cliff to the west of the Castle (which would have been invisible) but in exchange one gets a splendid birds-eye view of the town. Immediately after crossing the railway line one turns right to go into Sherborne. But if you keep on along the main road you come to a set of traffic lights admitting you to the fast and crowded A30. Turning left in the direction of Yeovil after about three or four miles, you take a small road to the right pointed to Trent.

Trent has not always belonged to Dorset but it does now and it is an acquisition worth having. Architecturally it is most distinguished. Its churchyard contains a most unusual medieval priest's house. And the church itself is top notch. It is one of the very few in the county to have a spire; and its un-Dorset character is further emphasised by a gorgeous wooden screen of the type usually associated with Devon. The carved bench-ends again are of a richness and abundance rivalled by no other church in the county. The north transept is largely taken up by the Phelips chantry full of decorous tombs of that family long eminent in the west country and penalised in the Civil War and the Interregnum for their inflexible Royalism.

For Trent is a Royalist shrine. It was here that the young Charles II, a hunted man after his defeat at the battle of Worcester in September 1651, took refuge for three weeks. He was sheltered in the manor house which, as it had belonged to the recusant Gerard family, had the useful security of a priest's hole. Anne Gerard, heiress to Trent, had married Francis Wyndham, a bold and enterprising Royalist colonel, who with his friend Colonel Robert Phelips undertook the arrangements for spiriting the King over to France. While waiting for the fruition of their plans Charles had the pleasure of seeing the villagers of Trent gathering in the churchyard to celebrate the news of his death which had just been brought by a trooper who claimed personally to have killed him. The buff coat he was wearing was, he declared, that which he had stripped from the corpse.

The story of the near miss and subsequent narrow shave at Charmouth and Bridport has already been told. The return to Trent must have tried the King's nerve. He left it and Dorset, finally, for Heale House just outside Salisbury on his way to the Sussex coast and success. On his triumphant return in 1660 those who had helped him were generously rewarded. It would be a plausible conjecture to see in the splendid late seventeenth-century Flemish pulpit, ornamented with a curious mixture of nude figures and scriptural scenes, a thank-offering from the monarch, commemorating his protection at Trent and his subsequent exile in Flanders with an acknowledgement of the nature of his personal pleasures. But it was in fact presented by an incumbent in early Victorian times.

The church is also the resting place of a prominent 1914–1918 war commander, General Rawlinson, perhaps unfairly reputed the ugliest man in the British Army. He was born in Trent Manor which, though perfectly preserved, is not open to the public. There is, however, hard by in this very pretty village an excellent pub.

Still in this north-western salient of Dorset are the two adjacent villages of Nether Compton and Over Compton, both stone-built and attractive. Over Compton contains an extraordinarily impressive statue of Robert Goodden, dated 1825. It has been given pride of place as the frontispiece to the first volume of the RCHM survey of the county. Goodden largely rebuilt the church and added the north chapel as a family pew. Nearby stands Compton House, an early Victorian replacement of the original destroyed by fire in 1827, the year before his death. The statue, which was clearly executed *ad vivum* and shows him in his everyday clothes, was kept boarded up with strict instructions that it should not be revealed until a year after his death. Michael Pitt-Rivers in the Shell Guide suggests that it is the work of Flaxman.

Over Compton is best approached from the west – that is to say either driving north from the roundabout just east of Yeovil which is, helpfully, pointed to Over Compton – or south from Trent on the Trent–Yeovil road. Coming round a sharp corner you will see some gate piers leading down an apparently private road. It is none the less metalled and tells you that it leads to the church and Compton House. Passing some new houses on your left you come to a proper lodge gate, inside which, if you are lucky, you will see a peacock contentedly preening himself on the grass of the park. Driving on, with the crunch of gravel under your tyres as you approach the cavernous but welcoming Jacobethan house, you will see signs directing you to the car park, for Compton House, enterprisingly, has entered on a new career as a butterfly museum, open daily from Easter to October.

The church, rebuilt by the admirable Goodden family, though only a stone's throw from the house is not simply its private chapel. There is a tomb to Onesiphorus Bicknell – how did he come by so pedantically classical a Christian name? – who died of a decline on June 4 1805. There is another to a member of the Bingham family who taught in the Sunday school. Like Tess's father he came from a branch of the family that had come down in the world. The inscription waves a hand in the direction of Bingham's Melcombe but is not mealy-mouthed about his own social position, indeed emphasises his truly liberal and gentle qualities contrasted with those of people who had slumbered away their time on the down of plenty. There is an enchanting little organ loft in the beautifully proportioned western tower with a Regency Gothick plaster ceiling. The exit road takes you through an even lovelier part of the park before politely bowing you on to the A30 with traffic hurtling past.

In the park is a column from the great sixteenth-century mansion of Clifton Maybank, a mile or two to the south-west the other side of the A30. This was the seat of the Horseys, whose tombs we have admired in Sherborne Abbey. In 1786 it was sold off to a number of bidders. A whole wing went to Montacute and bits and pieces are to be found as far away as Wiltshire. Fortunately the substantial remaining wing with a considerable range of interesting and beautiful outbuildings was restored to life as a private house early in the twentieth century. There is a good view of it from the road leading from Stoford to Bradford Abbas; but the best, if necessarily fugitive, is that from the enchanted railway line from Weymouth to Bristol, a journey that cannot be made without delight.

Stoford and Bradford Abbas have been somewhat engulfed by development. Bradford has a notable church, battlemented, with a fine western tower and a number of beautiful features. But Sherborne and Yeovil, particularly Yeovil, are breathing down their necks.

XII

Between Sherborne and Dorchester

1. Cerne and its neighbours

There are several routes one might take from Sherborne to Dorchester, all of them pleasant. And there are a number of places lying in between these roads which are even pleasanter.

Perhaps it is best to start with the main road, the A352. The first village, Longburton, has a certain charm but it can hardly be blamed for not having foreseen the car and the articulated lorry. Its long, twisting, narrow street never seems at ease. But down at its far end, standing a little back from the road, is the parish church of St James which contains some gaily coloured early seventeenth-century tombs. In spite of the assortment of skulls, bones and other full frontal statements of mortality that are gloatingly exhibited on the lower berth of Sir John Fitzjames's sleeper (he and his wife, decorously clad, he in armour, she in a ruff and gown, occupy the upper) the effect is almost that of a merry-go-round at a fair. There appears to be no attempt to portray character, still less to suggest grief or solemn reflections on eternity. Wealth, worldly importance, and the pleasures they bring, not least those of colour and comfort, seem to be the lesson we are taught.

> As I sat in the café I said to myself
> They may talk as they please about what
> they call pelf
> How pleasant it is to have money, heigh-ho
> How pleasant it is to have money.

The adjoining tomb is similarly cheerful: indeed, even more so, since instead of the ossuary on the lower bunk we have the grave bearded figure of Thomas Winston, and above him his son and daughter-in-law. One of their daughters, Sarah Winston, married John Churchill of nearby Glanvilles Wootton and *their* son, Sir Winston Churchill, was the father of John, first Duke of Marlborough and the ancestor of the statesman who saved his country in 1940. The inscription, interestingly, claims the descent of the Winstons from 'many ancient and noble howses both British & English'.

It is well worth obtaining the key of this church – directions are clearly given in the porch – not only for the monuments but also for the remarkably fine fifteenth-century glass in the north aisle, one panel of which, most unusually, shows the virgin in the act of breast-feeding the child, while a priest, host in hand, looks benignly on. The story of the recovery of the glass is admirably told in a leaflet available in the church. The whole lot was gaily knocked out in 1874 and most of it thrown away. But some was wrapped up in a newspaper and put in a box which was rediscovered by brilliant scholarly detective work exactly a century later.

Pressing on down the unusually straight well-wooded road, one suddenly becomes aware of a church standing alone in a field to one's right. Investigation of this phenomenon reveals that it is Holnest and that in spite of the absence of any visible population, services are still regularly held there. Evensong on a winter's night must be quite something as the church is still lit by candles held in metal arched candlesticks over each cream-coloured box pew (the first Sunday in the month at 6.30 p.m.). The key is kept at a cottage on the road that turns left to Glanvilles Wootton about a quarter of a mile further on, immediately opposite the decayed gates of the vanished mansion of Holnest Park.

At the rather boring little village of Middlemarsh the road divides, offering you parallel routes to Dorchester. If you stick on the A352 you find yourself climbing a romantic wooded hill called Lyon's Gate with an incongruous breaker's yard and some scruffy-looking wooden buildings suddenly emerging and, mercifully, as suddenly receding as though they had never been. The road narrows and twists into the tiny village of Minterne Magna, most beautifully set.

Minterne, not Sherborne which belongs to the Wingfield-Digbys, is the seat of the Digby family. The explanation of this is said to be found in the colourful career of Lady Ellenborough. The captivating and talented daughter of Admiral Sir Henry Digby, she was divorced by Act of Parliament in 1830 from her outraged husband, on the grounds of her adultery with Prince von Schwarzenberg. Lord Ellenborough fought a duel with him and received damages of £25,000 in an action for *crim. con.*

Lady Ellenborough then became the mistress of Ludwig I of Bavaria, before marrying in November 1832 his Prime Minister, who committed suicide when she deserted him. Her third marriage was to an Arab sheikh who was serving, somewhat improbably, as a general in the Greek army. She retired with him to Damascus, dying there in her seventy-fifth year while apparently contemplating a final elopement with her Dragoman.

These distant excitements had repercussions in Dorset. When the last Earl Digby, who was unmarried, died in 1856 the barony descended to his cousin, Admiral Digby's son and heir, the brother of Lady Ellenborough. But he left the Sherborne estates to his sister's son, George Wingfield-Baker who changed his name to Wingfield-Digby.

Minterne House is a bold Edwardian house not open to the public, but the gardens, which are imaginatively landscaped and unfussily maintained, are. The spring is their best season but they are always charming and give you a sight of Dorset landscape at one of its most beautiful passages. The little church, opening its west door direct on to the main road, is an unusual mixture of perpendicular (chancel), early seventeenth century (north chapel) and Regency (western tower). It is dominated – perhaps overwhelmed would be a better word – by the jumbo monuments in the north chapel. They too lose some of their effect by being shoved into a space too small for them but they are undeniably worth looking at. One of them is to Marlborough's brother, General Charles Churchill, so that we are reminded again of the Dorset roots of this military and political dynasty.

Winding southward your attention is drawn – as people say in aggrieved letters to newspapers – to the huge, and in every sense crude, figure of the Giant cut out of the turf in the chalk hillside to your left. You are nearing Cerne Abbas.

Who is the Giant and when does he date from? No one knows. He is not documented until the eighteenth century, so that if he is, as some conjecture, a Roman representation of Hercules with his club, generations of mute inglorious Cerne Abbasers must have kept scooping out the encroaching weeds and grass through the Middle Ages and the times of the Tudors and Stuarts. No doubt the explicitness of the rendering would have satisfied their far from prudish tastes. But the Victorian clergy, having tasted of the tree of knowledge of good and evil, felt that the fig-leaves of neglect were to be welcomed. They did not, as we see, get their way.

Cerne Abbas itself is one of Dorset's most visited villages. In summer the streets are jammed with cars and coaches, the pavements thronged with holidaymakers. If solitude is a necessary ingredient of your pleasures you will not turn off into the village but either step on it towards Dorchester or turn off to the right where a steep climb brings you to a hilltop with splendid views, both back towards the Giant or over towards the lovely hills of West Dorset. There is a track running along the ridge which makes a particularly agreeable walk.

But if you turn left into Cerne there is a lot to see. Its domestic architecture though variegated is harmonious. There are some pleasant brick buildings of the late seventeenth or early eighteenth century as well as the stone of the monastic survivals such as the tithe barn, the cob and thatch ubiquitous in Dorset and the stone and flint banding one associates with East Anglia.

The abbey which gave the place its name and its importance

has left only fringe buildings – but its fringe alone is evidence of its wealth. The guest house, the richly decorated porch to the abbot's lodging, the abbey farm and the tithe barn already mentioned, and the name Abbey Street are the only evidence of the vanished church. However, Abbey Street itself with its medieval houses and the great parish church of St Mary with its fine perpendicular tower makes an acceptable substitute.

The interior of the church is rewarding: Early English chancel with a fine stone screen; painted texts on the walls as at Puddletown; and even some traces of medieval wall painting. A most impressive wooden screen under the tower is dated 1749, but it has all the weight and deliberation of seventeenth-century work.

Cerne takes its name from the little river in whose valley it lies. Besides the village proper, it has its dependencies of Up Cerne and Nether Cerne. You will have passed the turn to Up Cerne on your right just after leaving Minterne. Had you taken it you would have twisted over a seductively wooded ridge down an even more bosky steep hill through which you catch the glitter of a lake below you to the left. This is the grand ornamental feature of a house that for all its spick and span condition seems lifeless. Architecturally, it is homely rather than beautiful: a large early seventeenth-century manor house much altered and restored in recent times. Yet there is something about it which suggests burglar alarms and security-guards rather than the cries of children at play. Its setting on the floor of its own glorious valley with hills, woods and cornfields rising round it is, nevertheless, enchanting.

Nether Cerne which you see from the road on your left as you head down the valley towards Dorchester, is hardly more than a pretty little medieval church. The road brings you to the Yeovil–Dorchester road, the A37, at Charminster, a pretty village with a notable church already mentioned at the end of Chapter V.

If you had taken the left-hand fork at Middlemarsh, you could have pursued your way southward parallel to the main road and never more than a mile or so from it. This road takes you along the top of the Cerne valley ridge and the only signs of habitation you will find are prehistoric – bar the odd farmhouse. It brings you into Dorchester keeping just to the east of Charminster. It is a very pretty road and there is less traffic.

A time-consuming but rewarding detour immediately after taking the left fork at Middlemarsh would be to turn sharp left again and zig-zag your way through farmyards and tumble-down cottages to Glanvilles Wootton, a place that quietly asserts a vanished grandeur. The church and the manor house are both well set back from the road. There are avenues and traces of a park. The manor house, much reduced in height and size, still retains its original name of Round Chimneys. It was here that John Churchill, father of Sir Winston, the Royalist soldier who was rewarded with court appointments under Charles II, lived after his marriage with Sarah Winston. After the Civil War both father and son faced heavy penalties for their Royalism; the son particularly, since he had borne arms for the King and had fought on to the end. He had been wounded at the storming of Bristol in 1645 and, without employment or much means of support, he spent the interregnum either at his father's house at Glanvilles Wootton or his wife's family house at Ashe, near Musbury, just over the Devon border. It was at Ashe that his son, the future Duke of Marlborough, was born in 1650.

Round Chimneys, which the Duke sold when he inherited, was even in Hutchins's time still quite a mansion though even then partly demolished and used as a farmhouse. 'This is one of the best planned and most comfortable houses which I have seen of the age of Elizabeth,' he wrote, 'and when complete must have been a very excellent gentleman's residence. The situation is pleasant and the surrounding grounds appear to have been formerly laid into gardens, fish-ponds, and every convenience for the residence of a man of fortune.'

The Glanvilles who gave the place its name had gone by the

end of the fourteenth century but they have left the beautiful south chapel of the parish church built by Sibyl de Glanville and endowed as a chantry in 1344.

From Glanvilles Wootton it is a short step to Buckland Newton, an imprecise geographical conception that oozes from one coagulation of houses to another without ever giving one the assurance that one has arrived. The Church of the Holy Rood and its surroundings are well worth finding though they are not on the direct route to anywhere else. The churchyard which slopes steeply downhill has splendid yews which make it all the more of a pity that the *tout ensemble* is marred by the concreting of the exterior. But the interior is very fine: Early English chancel; perpendicular nave with a high arcade striding down it. There are interesting Norman and Saxon carvings on both the exterior and interior keystone of the door by which you enter in the south porch.

Immediately above the church is a rather grand and unusual house: seventeenth-century, reconstituted in the Regency.

From Buckland Newton the direct way to Dorchester is by the road from Sturminster which passes through Alton Pancras and the Piddle valley already described.

If Buckland Newton is well hidden – or rather the interesting part of it – what can one say of the defences which the village of Folke has successfully maintained against the motor car and the march of mind? Only the most dedicated map-reading would enable you to approach it from the southern wild of Glanvilles Wootton. Better go back to the start and take the Sturminster turn a mile or so out of Sherborne on the A352 and then take a well concealed right turn about 300 yards beyond an extremely good pub called The Three Elms. You will then find yourself passing the Folke Golf Centre (one wonders that it is not called the Folke Golf Care Centre). But after that you have, for the moment, done with the late twentieth century. Some tall trees, a pretty cottage, a farm and then a large much-restored seventeenth-century manor house and beyond it, down a bewitching cul-de-sac which peters into a bridleway is the church of St Lawrence.

The interior is astonishing. Miraculously even the Victorian restorers worked in the idiom of the early seventeenth century, when the whole church had been lavishly reconstructed and furnished. The screen is a bold and original work; but even more so the graceful screen-doorway by which one enters the north aisle from the middle of the nave. All is of a piece: the font and its cover, the pulpit and the stand for the hour glass by which the preacher might regulate his edification. This is the Church of England over which, in their different ways, Archbishop Abbot and Archbishop Laud presided: the Church of George Herbert and Lancelot Andrewes. A visit to Folke helps the imagination to enter the pre-Civil War England pictured by Clarendon in his two exiles and by J. H. Shorthouse in the novel *John Inglesant*.

It is hard to think of another church like Folke. But only a few miles away there is another, almost of the same date: a bare twelve years in it, even more perfect and even more beautiful but different. This is Leweston, which you reach by taking a right-hand fork as you approach Longburton coming from Sherborne and then take a right-hand turn, well marked by a notice, into the park. The house is now a convent school, a transformation somewhat stridently asserted by a block of buildings which would be well enough in Harlesden but are out of key with the soft beauties of the landscape in which they are set and with the quiet dignity of the buildings they adjoin. Leweston is an uninspired but decent late eighteenth-century stone-built country house. The depressed arches of its windows weaken rather than lighten the effect of its front. But it is not the house that concerns us so much as the exquisite chapel standing fifty yards to the left and in front of it.

Folke's preservation is wonderful enough: but even there the seventeenth-century pews have been stained with that dark varnish so frequently associated with public worship. In Leweston the natural colour of the pews rising to the authoritative dignity of the pulpit in the south-east angle of the chapel glints silver-grey. The rounded bench-ends of the pews each have their hat-peg behind them. Even the clock in the western porch which you hear measuring out the moments of your visit has its neat little wooden pit, like a refined umbrella stand, for the clock-weights to nest in. The inscription on the stained glass tells you that it was built by Sir John Fitzjames to replace the chapel which had fallen into disrepair. He had married the daughter of the last Leweston whose graceful monument we have admired in Sherborne Abbey.

A modern tablet in the porch informs us that Thomas Ken spent the last winter of his life at Leweston and must often have worshipped here. Ken, a non-juror who had been deprived of the bishopric of Bath and Wells in 1691, passed the last twenty years of his life as a guest at Longleat where he died. His sojourn at Leweston was no doubt occasioned by his host's daughter having married the Fitzjames of the day. His morning and evening hymns,

> Awake, my soul, and with the sun
> Thy daily course of duty run

and

> Glory to thee, my God, this night

are still familiar in English worship. He was an accomplished musician as well as a liturgist. But he is perhaps best remembered for his moral courage in refusing the hospitality of the close at Winchester to Nell Gwynn when the Court was paying a visit there. His stout-heartedness did him no harm with the monarch who, at the next episcopal vacancy, declared that he would give it 'to the little black man who refused poor Nelly a lodging'. Seventeenth-century piety is richly evoked at Holy Trinity, Leweston.

XIII
Between Sherborne and Dorchester
2. Western approaches

The countryside between the A352 Sherborne to Dorchester road and the A37 from Yeovil is little disturbed by through traffic. There are a couple of very beautiful but not at all fast east-west routes, from Evershot to Minterne and from Cattistock to Cerne, but north-south drivers will take the A37 or the A352. There is thus a cone of tranquillity with its apex at Dorchester and its base along the Yeovil–Sherborne line. And to the west of it, another similar cone bounded by the A37 and the A356 to Crewkerne.

We have already intruded on the first by our expedition to Leweston. If, on leaving the park, we turn right the road runs through pleasant if unexciting country to Tatnell Corner. If you then choose the right turn it will take you to Leigh – pronounced like the unparliamentary word for untruth – an inoffensive but uninspired place, and then to Chetnole which also lacks character. But Yetminster a few miles to the north is a charming village with a most attractive church. It is high and light, showing to advantage the original colour remaining on much of the stonework and in particular on the rafters of the north aisle. There is a fine brass on the south wall, depicting Sir John Horsey, the builder of Clifton Maybank, and his wife.

A mile away is the irresistibly named Ryme Intrinseca.

'Rime Intrinseca, Fontmell Magna, Sturminster Newton & Melbury Bubb'.

Had Sir John Betjeman visited these places when he wrote this early poem, or were the place-names chosen, as he tells us the proper names in the refrain were, 'merely for their euphony'? We know that A. E. Housman's knowledge of Shropshire was intuited from ordnance survey maps rather than founded on personal contact with the farm labourers through whom his Muse addresses us. Betjeman subsequently sat on the Royal Commission whose survey of Dorset's Historical Monuments has been gratefully alluded to. But he was not among those who compiled the first volume in which this pretty little village is described. He certainly would have savoured the eccentricity of the dedication of the church to St Hypolite, an early bishop of Ostia – an association almost as impenetrable as the choice of twin towns in our own day. It is a church of some charm and interest but the Victorians have given it the works.

But reverting to Tatnell Corner, and turning left instead of right, you find yourself heading towards Hermitage and the beautiful wooded hill beyond it, Dogbury Gate. This is bewitching country for walking and riding; and at Three Gates, on the road from Tatnell Corner, you pass the Leigh Equestrian Centre which maintains high standards and provides escorted rides for those who want to see this exciting part of the country where wild flowers flourish and the obbligato of the internal combustion engine is happily absent.

At the foot of the range of hills on which Dogbury lies are the tiny and extremely pretty villages of Hilfield and Batcombe. The setting of Batcombe church is particularly delightful. Both from it and from Hilfield narrow lanes twist up the side of the hill to join the very beautiful road that runs along the crest from Evershot to Minterne. There is a notably well-placed picnic site with ample parking, commanding splendid views. There is no motor road southward so, unless you are on foot or on horseback, a descent of one of the main roads is necessary until you meet the other, only slightly less beautiful, east-west road from Cattistock to Cerne. If you turn off this to the south you will come, by a most companionable stream, to Sydling St Nicholas, a place of great charm.

Both John Newman and Jo Draper are good on the domestic architecture of this surprisingly grand village. Unlike anywhere else in Dorset it has the air of being a fairly important place on a fairly important route without in fact being either. It has always been the seat of rich or prominent families. The branch of the Husseys, established here by the early seventeenth century, suffered for their Royalism. At the beginning of the eighteenth century the estate was bought by Sir William Smith, one of a long line of Exeter merchants whose most successful member, Sir George Smith, numbered among his many daughters the mother of George Monck, the key figure in Charles II's restoration, and the wife of Sir Bevil Grenville, Hopton's companion in arms as leader of the Cavaliers in the south-west. They lived in the handsome house adjoining the church, in which their monuments are a prominent feature.

The church itself is refreshing. Light and spacious, its perpendicular architecture is especially well set off by the abundance of clear glass which also enables you to appreciate the generous park-like landscape in which it is set.

Pressing on southward down the pretty valley of the Sydling Water as our stream has now become, we reach the A37 at Grimstone and turn northward, away from Dorchester, to explore the second cone. Still on the main road the first village, Frampton, has a particularly interesting church bang on the street. The Tower, a curiosity dating from 1695 discussed in all the books, is the creation of an amateur architect, a member of the Browne family whose monuments dominate the north aisle. They were lords of the manor from the time of Henry VI down to the Great Reform Bill and one of them, John Browne, was returned as member for the County to the Long Parliament when Charles I created a vacancy by calling up George Digby to the House of Lords.

John Browne proved a very different representative. He had married into the Trenchards of Wolfeton and had been a member of John White's New England company. A zealous Parliament man, he tactfully died in 1659, allowing his son to serve the restored monarchy as Sheriff. John Browne's father, Sir John Browne, had served both Elizabeth and James I in that capacity and appears to have lost his life in the military and diplomatic fiasco of the expedition against the Isle of Rhé in 1627.

The house they lived in has long vanished. But Jo Draper points out that the lop-sided appearance of the village results from the demolition of the houses on the Frampton Park side of the road to give the great house a grander prospect.

The road follows the Frome valley up to Maiden Newton, a furtive-looking town whose maidenhead was surely lost some centuries ago. But a turn to the right as you come in takes you to the Church of St Mary, which stands apart as if distancing itself from the down-at-heel, depressing little place to which it belongs. It has a dignity and grace that rises above the trendiness and poor taste of its interior arrangements. There is a handsome central tower but no north transept though the masonry of the exterior suggests past alterations. In the north wall of the nave is a Saxon doorway, blocked on the exterior wall by a Norman arch. The flowing decorated tracery of the west window is beautiful.

We here leave the A37 to ramble up the remoter reaches of the Frome. Chilfrome has charm without any adventitious architectural advantages. But its neighbour, Cattistock, which lends its name to a famous hunt, has several. The cottages at its centre are particularly attractive and the Church of St Peter and St Paul, whose tower dominates the place, is as beautiful as it is unexpected. Here in the sleepiest part of sleepy Dorset is a highly imaginative and effective piece of nineteenth-century architecture, the creation, almost entirely, of George Gilbert Scott *père et fils*. Unlike so much good Victorian Gothic it is not imitative. There is no medieval tower that provides a pattern for the uncompromising perpendicularity of Cattistock tower. One is vaguely reminded of Gloucester and Malvern, but neither is so strict, so severe. The resemblance is a family one.

Inside the tower is bold and dashing in the use of colour and ornament. The Temple Morris font cover is a breathtaking ecclesiological folly, as magnificently, as defiantly, purposeless as the bridge at Blenheim. And how it comes off! There are other beauties, notable among them the William Morris window in the south nave aisle. Not that the church is rich only in its artistic quality. It is evidently a living space of worship and the Battle ensigns from the Hunt class destroyer HMS *Cattistock* are proudly displayed.

Cattistock church must have a chequered history. It was largely rebuilt in 1630 by the then rector, so that the neglect of the eighteenth and early nineteenth centuries must have been gross to require so complete a reconstruction by the Scotts. Perhaps simony, the buying up of the patronage in order to present oneself or one's relations to the living, had something to do with it. At any rate there is a story of this.

In 1698 the incumbent, who had bought the right of presentation and, perhaps, used it in his own favour, died, leaving two daughters as his co-heiresses. One of them, who was engaged to a clergyman, wished to present the living to her lover. Whether she did not offer her sister enough to buy out her interest, or whether there were family reasons for preventing the marriage, they found difficulty in reaching an agreement. While they were haggling the wily diocesan bishop perceived an opening for his chaplain. A lapse in the ministry would allow him to nominate and institute his own candidate. The chaplain lurked in the offing. As the day dawned the bishop appeared in his canonicals and the first the heiresses knew of their miscalculation was hearing the church bells rung to celebrate the installation. And the new rector reigned for *fifty-nine years*! Collapse, as *Punch* would have said, of stout party. But at least the course of true love seems, after this initial rough weather, to have run smooth because the successor to this parsonical Methuselah was the son of the lady and the gentleman who had muffed their chance. He, in his turn, was succeeded by his half-brother.

Leaving Cattistock, if you fork right-handed up the Frome you will pass what used to be the two great houses of the parish: Chalmington, on the right, which was largely reconstructed in the nineteenth century, and, about half a mile further on, Chantmarle, which sounds like the title of a novel by Daphne du Maurier. Chantmarle was built, pretty well to his own specifications, by Sir John Strode in 1612. Sir John was a younger brother of the owner of Parnham and, like the rest of the family, a devout Puritan. He has left an account of the building of the house, which included its own chapel, and the ceremony of consecration to which in those happy days, a generation before the Civil War, he entertained the principal Dorset nobs: a Strangways from Melbury, a Trenchard from Wolfeton and so on.

The house is now a Police Training College. Roughly handled in the late nineteenth and early twentieth centuries, it is still beautiful. Sir John employed two experienced masons from Ham Hill and the house he built was entirely of that lovely stone.

A little further on, just before the road joins the A37, is the little village of Frome St Quintin at the centre of which is a particularly handsome late eighteenth-century house, built, for once, of brick. The church, which I have not visited, stands on its own in the fields just off the road. According to Michael Pitt-Rivers in the Shell Guide it 'suffered ruthlessly at its restoration in 1879'.

But if on leaving Cattistock you choose the left fork and decline the invitation of the direct road to Evershot you will find yourself passing the Wraxalls. Lower Wraxall has a small medieval church with some superior verse inscriptions on the monuments to William Laurence and his wife. William Laurence's father built the manor house at Higher Wraxall, clearly visible from the road, about 1620–1630. William was a successful lawyer who married the sister of his neighbour Colonel Sydenham the Parliamentary commander, and was himself a prominent Republican, serving the Cromwellian régime in Scotland as a judge. He wrote learnedly on marriage – Anthony Wood, a bigoted Royalist, suggests that he was prompted to do so by the infidelities of his attractive wife – and on primogeniture. Perhaps it was the association of ideas with Milton's well-known treatise on Divorce that led Wood to suggest that he belonged to the same family as Milton's close friend and fellow Republican Henry Lawrence, but there appears to be no foundation for this. Anyway there is no echo of marital discord in the inscriptions.

The next village, Rampisham, is delightful. Small, secluded, unselfconscious, free from the suburban improvements that too often attend the second home or the establishments of the retired, it nestles in its valley. Above it, on Rampisham Hill, are the transmitters of the World Service of the BBC. Down here, the world is well lost.

But if the depth of the countryside stirs a craving for the metropolitan, take the road for Evershot which hesitates between the status of large village and very small town. Perhaps the former just has the edge; but there are plenty of places to eat and drink and even stay. Summer Lodge shares with Plumber Manor an established reputation for Lucullan meals and expert, unobtrusive hospitality. It is, naturally, not cheap and it is best to book in advance. In the very attractive main street there is a handsome inn with a large yard with plenty of parking. It has a restaurant and you can stay there but it also has a wide range of bar food and plenty of room outside if you like eating in the open air.

At the foot of the main street the road swerves deferentially to the right so as not to intrude on the Park of Melbury House. It is a wonderful Park, perhaps the most beautiful in the county, and not often open. When it is, you can drive past the house which lies at its centre and visit the tiny church of Melbury Sampford which is really its domestic chapel though it stands a hundred yards from it a little lower down the hill. It is rather dark, cluttered with ornament, more of a mortuary chapel than a place of worship. Indeed the monuments it houses, from the fourteenth to the nineteenth centuries, are notable; especially two fifteenth-century alabasters.

The setting of the house is glorious. Seen from across the lake, the great trees and garden shrubs framing the gentle rise of lawn on which sits, serenely, the great palace stretching from the late seventeenth-century wing on the right to Salvin's enormous tower with its adjacent library built in the form of a medieval hall, it fills the mind with pleasure. But if you were standing on the terrace of that garden front with your back to the house, the rising slope of the park itself would be no less exhilarating.

The view across the lake does not do justice to the earlier parts of this complicated architectural composition. In particular the most original feature of the Tudor house, the Lantern Tower, a hexagon with windows in each of its sides, is relegated to the background. It is more conspicuous as you approach the house by the drive. You then have on your right a low two-storey modest building of the mid to late seventeenth century that would be an almshouse if it had ground floor windows and front doors, but is in fact the east wing of the stable block. In front of you is the north front of the east wing added to the house in the reign of William and Mary when the calamities of the Civil Wars, which had destroyed the main family house at Abbotsbury, and the swingeing financial penalties imposed by the Commonwealth were things of the past. Sir John Strangways had been exchanged after being taken prisoner at Abbotsbury and had once again taken up arms for the King. He and his son were among the hard-core of Royalists who surrendered at the storming of Sherborne Castle. Appealed to for help when the fugitive Charles II was sheltering at Trent in 1651, he had sent him £100 in gold – say £10,000 in present values – but had regarded himself as too much a marked man to be of any active assistance.

The east wing is not great architecture but the rooms that compose it are airy, light and gracious without the affectation of the exterior where provincial architects were applying

Renaissance ornament without understanding it. The plasterers and carpenters, by contrast, were working in an idiom in which they were at home. When the new wing was built the entrance was by the east front. The drive came over a small lake by a bridge. But in the next century Capability Brown turned the axis of the house through ninety degrees by removing the lake from the east to the south side of the house, thus creating the wonderful prospect with which we began. The entrance was then transferred to the north where it has remained.

The culminating addition a century later was Salvin's enormous west wing and tower, returning stylistically to the Tudor origins of the house. And when all is said and done it is the hexagon tower with its exhilarating views over a particularly lovely tract of this lovely country that is the architectural high point in every sense of this splendid house.

It is remarkable that the house has always passed by descent. The Strangways line issued in an heiress who, on her marriage to one of the two sons of Sir Stephen Fox, added her surname to his. Sir Stephen is a notable example of the pliancy of the English class system. He had been a choirboy at Salisbury who obtained employment as a steward in a noble household from which he passed to the royal service. During Charles II's years of exile when the Court was on its uppers, Clarendon, Charles's political adviser, persuaded the King to entrust the management of his household to this enterprising young man. So well did he manage the embarrassed finances of his extravagant and self-indulgent master that he was rewarded at the Restoration with offices that enabled him to amass an enormous fortune. Premature death had robbed him of his first wife and the sons she had borne him so that in his old age he took a second wife fifty years his junior and fathered two sons; Stephen, who married the Strangways heiress and was created Earl of Ilchester, and Henry, who married the daughter of the Duke of Richmond. Henry, a formidable and avaricious politician, later created Lord Holland, was the father of

Charles James Fox. Father and son between them personify the brilliant Whig world of politics and letters whose centre was Holland House. It reached its apogee in the time of Henry's grandson, the third Lord Holland who died in 1840.

What has all this to do with Melbury? The Fox cousinhood was a close one. Succeeding generations of the Ilchester and Holland branches were very much at home in each other's houses. With the extinction of the Holland line, the splendid possessions of Holland House, its wonderful library and its superb collection of Whig portraits found a home in Melbury. Salvin's great hall was built to house the books (they have had, at last, to be sold to pay death duties) and the pictures, fortunately, were brought down here for safety in 1939 before the Blitz destroyed Holland House a year later. It was not the only great house to be embalmed in Melbury. There are rooms which owe their plasterwork, their silk damask wallpaper or their Mortlake tapestries to Redlynch, the Fox house in Somerset. It is a triumph that so much has survived and that it is still in a house that is lived in and valued by its inheritors.

The portraits, in which the house is rich, illustrate both the political traditions with which it has been associated. There are Van Dycks of Charles I and Henrietta Maria, portraits of Charles II as a young man and of Sir Stephen Fox. There is the whole gamut of Whiggery from its early martyrs such as the second Capel Earl of Essex. A small but most interesting Wotton of Sir Robert Walpole in Richmond Park commemorates its longest serving and most successful prime minister. There is a whole room full of portraits of the particular friends of the third Lord Holland and his tempestuous wife. And there is of course a wonderfully fresh and vivid portrait of Charles James Fox. He appears too with his beautiful cousin, Lady Sarah Lennox, in another charming portrait on which Lord David Cecil centres his evocation of the house.

There are two other Melburys with which we may close this chapter: Melbury Osmond and Melbury Bubb. Osmond is due north of the great house but is reached by turning on to the

A37 towards Yeovil and then turning off to the left. It is on its own, on the road to nowhere, and clearly likes it. It even retains a water splash – there are several of these in Dorset: the most conspicuous being the one just north of Sydling St Nicholas on the east-west road from Cattistock to Cerne. Altogether a charming village.

Even more successful in holding the outside world at bay is Melbury Bubb. So secluded is it that you need an Ordnance Survey map to find it. Although both Michael Pitt-Rivers and Jo Draper describe it well and give map references that would be right if the place were shown, it has cunningly effaced itself from the maps in their books. It is only about a mile or two due east of Melbury House as the crow flies, but the bird would have to retain altitude enough to cross Bubb Down, under which the village nestles. Even 'village' is a misnomer. It consists of a fine manor house, rebuilt in the early seventeenth century and a charming church rebuilt, except for the tower, in 1854. It incorporates some late medieval glass in its windows but its unforgettable feature is its font. To make it out you must first recognise that the vivid and striking relief with which it is ornamented is upside down. What on earth is it? Clearly it was not designed as a font. Most authorities agree in identifying it as Saxon work and deduce that it was part of the shaft of a Saxon cross which was then hollowed out and re-used as a font.

Perhaps. But guesswork is free and to me the design suggests something from the eastern end of the Mediterranean: Syriac or some such. How it fetched up in this hidden church among the supremely English beauties of the Dorset countryside is a pleasing puzzle, all the more so for being insoluble.

XIV
Westward to Forde Abbey

The northern border of the county as one heads westward
follows no thoroughfare. What it does follow, fairly faithfully
if sometimes at a mile or two's distance, is the very beautiful
railway line between the still active Yeovil junction and the
extinct junction at Chard. Both these towns are themselves just
across the county boundary.

Only a mile west of Melbury Osmond, across a wooded hill
over which there is no road, is the marvellously secret little
church of Lewcombe. So anxious is it to exclude prying eyes
that it even has the alias of East Chelborough. The best way of
finding it is probably to go out hunting with the Cattistock
when hounds are meeting in these parts, but for those to whom
this is impossible or improper a long circuit is necessary. It lies
to the east of the remote and rather beautiful road that runs
roughly north and south from Closworth to Rampisham. You
take what looks like a private road into someone's park and
press on, with increasing improbability, until there, couched
like a deer, you see the little church with a handsome small
house just to the right of it.

Its simplicity is worthy of its setting. A small, late medieval
building washed and brushed up in the eighteenth century,
with a bellcote added over the west front. Inside, it is a delight.
Nothing showy and everything effective, above all the circular
east window, whose tracery and glass are unlike anything else
in the county. What date is it? Eighteenth-century says the
RCHM tersely, before turning to the windows in the north and
south walls which, though perfectly in keeping, are not nearly
so arresting. Edwardian, says Michael Pitt-Rivers boldly.

Pevsner in the Penguin admits himself foxed but summarises the architectural evidence with the subtlety and penetration to be expected of him.

Lewcombe is still in use, unlike its pretty little neighbour to the east of the A37, Stockwood, whose setting in deep woodland with an elegant cottage to keep it company is somewhat similar. Stockwood is the smallest church in Dorset and can hardly fail to charm.

To keep south of the Somerset border requires persistence and perversity – there are so many exciting and enticing places just the other side of it. But passing through Halstock, a rather diffuse village with an uncharacteristically colourless Pugin church, you can either fork left for Corscombe, a much more compact, well-knit place of some charm, or right for South Perrott which has a large cruciform church of some interest (not, it must be admitted, to be compared with its outstandingly attractive sister, North Perrott, across the county boundary) and a fine medieval farmhouse. Seaborough, overlooking the valley of the infant Axe, has a remote, intriguingly forsaken air. Like Blackdown and Birdsmoor Gate, it has a bracing, almost East Coast quality. This is an uncharacteristic part of Dorset.

But it contains one of the county's greatest treasures. Forde Abbey, open to the public on Wednesday and Sunday afternoons in the season, is in the same class as, though utterly different from, Cranborne and Melbury. Slightly to the east of Chard junction – at which no train now stops – you can catch a glimpse of it from the line that gives you a better idea of its situation than any of the approaches by road. It lies, as so many Cistercian abbeys do, remote in a river valley of great natural beauty. It is a gloss on the vanity of human wishes, even when consciously directed towards subordination to the divine will, that the Cistercian order, which was founded to express simplicity and austerity, has left us the richest and most elaborate monastic buildings of any. Nowhere is this more conspicuously true than at Forde since there is not one stone left on another of the abbey church and even its exact site is a matter of conjecture. Probably it was under the splendid lawns that stretch in front of the house. What does remain however, and that in a high state of preservation, is the magnificent porch tower and the great hall built by Abbot Chard as the clouds were gathering for the dissolution of the monastic houses. No one would guess from the pride and confidence of the architecture that the foundations of the whole system were about to be destroyed.

In 1539, when the blow fell, Abbot Chard's operations were still in full swing. The cloister was still unfinished. It is possible to see how far the masons had got because, along with Chard's tower and great hall, the building was incorporated into the handsome house which, a century later, was acquired and extended by Edmund Prideaux. The intervening owners seem to have left Chard's work more or less as it was. No doubt they made a pretty penny, stripping the church of its glass and woodwork and selling off its fabric. But the Forde Abbey which we see today is, as Henry Thorold points out in his Collins *Guide to the Ruined Abbeys of England, Scotland and Wales* (1993), the work of two men, Chard and Prideaux.

His description of the house, looking at its south front, conveys its quality and assigns its origins with easy mastery:

... Chard's late Perpendicular porch-tower, tall and dramatic, with its two-storeyed oriel window above the entrance arch, all elaborately decorated. To its left is Chard's Great Hall, with its long Perpendicular windows. But to its right Prideaux built a new centrepiece, broader than Chard's tower, but lower, and with its later eighteenth-century loggia projecting several feet from the front and its grand seventeenth-century windows lighting Prideaux's first-floor saloon, this forms an important frontispiece. To the right stands the north range of Chard's cloister, incomplete at the Dissolution. Above this Prideaux added a series of seventeenth-century rooms on the first floor. On the far right is the Norman chapterhouse, dressed up externally in seventeenth-century style. To this Prideaux added an upper storey, so that it could balance the tall block which he contrived at the other end out of Chard's new abbot's lodging. The whole façade is battlemented – thus making a remarkable unity out of all these disparate parts.

Who was Prideaux and how did he come to be the owner, even to an extent the creator, of this perfectly glorious house? The second half of the question is easily answered: he bought it in 1649, the year of Charles I's execution. That he was in a position to do so at such a moment tells us, if we needed to be told, that he was a Parliament man. And how! He sat for Lyme Regis in the Long Parliament and was a member of whatever assembly continued to meet at St Stephen's, the Rump, the Barebones Parliament, and the Protectorate Parliaments, until his death in August 1659. More than that, he was one of the three members appointed by the House in 1643 as Commissioners of the Great Seal, that ultimate source of English legality. He was in fact a chancery lawyer and a very successful one.

Exceptionally well placed to profit from the successive phases of the Civil War and Interregnum, he never put a foot wrong and yet avoided the reputation of insincerity or time-serving. How did he do it?

In the first place he was an aristocrat. The Prideaux of Prideaux Castle in Cornwall were an ancient family. His own father, a Devon squire, had also been a prosperous lawyer and sent his son to Cambridge and the Inns of Court. In the second place his political and religious convictions were, without either hypocrisy or violence, congruent to the circumstances in which he found himself. He was a Presbyterian and he was wholeheartedly opposed to everything the King and Queen stood for. So far, so good. Like most lawyers he was, too, averse from the clash of arms. With his friend Bulstrode Whitelocke he was one of the Commissioners sent by Parliament to the so-called Treaty of Uxbridge when a last attempt was made to end the Civil War by negotiation. Yet Clarendon, who was one of the Royalist team at that fixture and an old personal friend of Whitelocke's, tells us that Prideaux, along with Sir Henry Vane, was one of the Politburo's men, sent to report on the others if they got too intimate with their old Royalist friends.

Certainly Prideaux was well in with the Cromwell-Vane-St John group who were filling the vacuum left by the death of Pym. In 1644 he had obtained the lucrative appointment of Postmaster. But when it became clear that the King was to be brought to trial he would have nothing to do with it. Nonetheless, a couple of months after the execution he was appointed Attorney-General and held office till his death. He shewed considerable adroitness in defending his monopoly of the posts for a number of years. After he eventually lost it he continued to make a large income from his Chancery work.

There was thus no need to spare expense in beautifying Forde. What would have happened if he had lived a few months longer and, as a thorough-going Rumper, might have backed Milton and those who thought as he did in a vain effort to prevent the Restoration, we do not know. But he had the tact to die with the same exquisite timing as he had lived, and Forde passed to his son. Had he, like his friend Whitelocke, made enough money to buy a country seat before the Civil War it would have certainly been vandalised by Royalist troops, as Whitelocke's was. But he bought at the right moment and we are his beneficiaries.

As we are of the present owner, who opens his house with the minimum of restrictive fuss. The contents and interior ornament are as interesting and beautiful as the architecture. Prideaux's grand staircase reminds us that by no means all Puritans disdained the arts of life, not to say its luxuries. At the beginning of the eighteenth century the Prideaux heiress, Edmund's grand-daughter, married a Gwyn in whose family the house remained till the middle of the nineteenth century. They did not always live there since at one point it was leased to Jeremy Bentham, the utilitarian philosopher who entertained here thinkers of a similar turn of mind such as John Stuart Mill. Was Thomas Love Peacock thinking of Forde when he wrote *Nightmare Abbey*, that wonderfully high-spirited attack on intellectual trendiness which he characterised as the March of Mind?

Bentham and Mill would both have had their noses too deep in books to have noticed the outstandingly fine gardens and grounds in which the modern visitor is free to wander. There is also a vast walled garden where you can pick your own fruit or buy plants from the nursery.

Forde is one of Dorset's treasures, not to be the less valued because it is purloined. For far the greater part of its history, certainly in Abbot Chard's or Edmund Prideaux's time, it belonged to Devon. It is a high point at which to bring this survey to an end.

XV
Reading about Dorset

In the course of writing this book I have made frequent and grateful allusion to John Newman and Nikolaus Pevsner's Dorset volume in the Penguin Buildings of England series, to Michael Pitt-Rivers' Shell Guide (in the brilliant series edited by John Betjeman and John Piper) and to Jo Draper's *Dorset: The Complete Guide*. Of these only the last is at the time of writing still in print, and what a boon it is. Design, printing and illustration leave nothing to be desired. The price is a bargain. The accurate and concise presentation of a great deal of information, much of it learned and out of the way, is achieved without the slightest touch of the patronising or the pedantic. The range justifies the definite article of the sub-title.

I have also found much of value in Arthur Oswald's *The Country Houses of Dorset* (Country Life, 1935, n.e. 1959). Lucid, scholarly, with excellent photographs and clear plans it is the best book on the subject. Lord David Cecil's delightful *Some Dorset Country Houses* carefully disclaims both in its title and in its introduction any pretence to a similar comprehensiveness but it is a book that anyone interested in the subject would wish to possess. Although it is out of print at the moment of writing I understand that its publishers, The Dovecote Press, intend to bring out a reprint. The Dovecote Press has an extensive list of books about Dorset which anyone interested in particular places or topics would do well to consult. The country houses open to the public, certainly those looked after by the National Trust, usually have clear and detailed guidebooks on sale.

The volumes of the RCHM are in a class by themselves.

Copious and minute, they are of course works of reference, not intended for continuous reading, still less for taking about on sight-seeing expeditions. The quality of production is admirable; and the large leaf-size gives all forms of illustration, from photographs to plans, an advantage which has been taken to the full. There is an amplitude, a spaciousness, about them that makes the reader feel that justice will be done to the subject though the heavens fall.

This quality is also present in the four stout volumes of Hutchins' *History of Dorset* reprinted with a new introduction in 1973. Unlike the RCHM, the Reverend John Hutchins did not have the resources of public finance either in the collection or the publication of his material. He was, it is true, supported and encouraged by private patrons. Indeed without such assistance he could never have embarked on so vast an undertaking. Every writer on the history of Dorset who has come after him has built on the foundations, the deep and strong foundations, laid by his often bitter labour.

For Hutchins' life was not the leisurely, ample existence of a Georgian country rector of scholarly tastes. From the title page we see that he was Rector of Holy Trinity in Wareham and of Swyre in the County of Dorset. Swyre even in the eighteenth century must have been a sinecure and Wareham, an ancient borough, must surely have been a good living. A picture begins to form in the mind of a comfortable, well-regulated household, its library and its cellar well-stocked, looking out on the world through tall sash-windows. Such an establishment would give a man of general curiosity perfect scope. And the *History and Antiquities of the County of Dorset* is generous, not to say profuse, in the information it imparts. Natural History, Archaeology and Prehistory, Buildings (of course), Inscriptions in churches and churchyards, Economic and Legal material from Domesday downwards, Topography in all its amplitude from Ptolemy to Hutchins' own time, Heraldry and Genealogy at the marvellous spread afforded by folio pages, Biography and Anecdote . . . the mind trails away in wonder.

His talk was like a stream which runs
  With rapid change from rocks to roses:
It slipp'd from politics to puns;
  It pass'd from Mahomet to Moses:
Beginning with the laws which keep
  The planets in their radiant courses,
And ending with some precept deep
  For dressing eels, or shoeing horses.

The Vicar of Praed's verses, whose hospitality and warmth of
sympathy matched the breadth of his interests, might seem a
plausible image of our author. Ease and a sunny, contented
nature with plenty to be contented about, above all intellectual
freedom to range wherever curiosity might lead, these supply
the rubicund tones of such a portrait. One sees why George
Orwell, asked to choose a period and situation other than his
own, said he would like to have been a country vicar in
eighteenth-century England.

Yet nothing could have been less true to what we know of
Hutchins. What was he like? Who, indeed, was he? A memoir of
him written by his friend and occasional collaborator, George
Bingham, the Rector of Pimperne, who was also for many years a
Fellow of All Souls, prefaces the second edition. Together with
the excellent introduction to the 1973 reprint written by Robert
Douch it supplies us with a sympathetic and convincing account.

Hutchins was born in 1698, the son and grandson of Dorset
clergymen. Apart from the four years he spent at Oxford, first
at Hart Hall (now merged into Hertford College) and then
Balliol, he lived all his life in Dorset, dying in 1773 at
Wareham, a year before the publication of the work to which
he had given his all. He was ordained deacon in 1722 and
priest in 1723, serving as curate at Buckland Newton and
perhaps briefly at other parishes for a starveling salary, before
being appointed curate of Milton Abbas. To this post was
added that of an usher (as teachers were then styled) at the
Grammar School there.

From this dates his career as Dorset's historian. The then

owner of Milton Abbey, Jacob Bancks, a cultivated and public-spirited bachelor, suggested to the young clergyman that he should write the history of the county and offered to help him with money and with introductions to his fellow squires, without which in those days before County Record Offices there was no hope of access to the principal local sources. Bancks, it will have been noticed, spelled his name with a 'c'. He had nothing to do with the Royalist owners of Corfe Castle and Kingston Lacy. His grandfather had arrived in this country as Swedish ambassador to Charles II and his father, apparently without discarding his Swedish nationality, had had a brief but distinguished career in the Royal Navy before marrying a daughter of John Tregonwell and thus acquiring the estate of Milton Abbas.

Jacob Bancks was directly responsible for Hutchins' first step towards financial independence by securing his presentation to the rectory of Swyre in 1729, and, indirectly through his friendship with the squire at Bingham's Melcombe, to the addition of that rectory in 1733. This enabled Hutchins to marry. Just before Christmas in that year he led to the altar the daughter of yet another Dorset rector and began on what was probably the happiest and most productive period of his life. His parochial duties cannot have taken up much of his time. And George Bingham makes it plain that he was a careful and conscientious parish priest rather than a steward of the divine mysteries who found his profession its own great reward. He was, in short, by nature and inclination a scholar. And the unreformed University of Oxford, that much maligned institution, had stimulated and educated these tastes. But it was then by its own constitution necessarily a clerical body. Almost all of its college and university appointments required their holders to be in holy orders and none of them except for the Heads of Houses and the Canons of Christ Church were permitted to marry. A rectory or vicarage was the recognised ambition of a learned man who had no inclination to celibacy. Not all such men were as scrupulous as Hutchins appears to have been in discharging the pastoral duties involved.

He seems to have been blessed, and certainly as we shall see his book was blessed, in his wife and in the daughter she bore him. For soon enough the sky began to darken over the prospect of the vast work that he had taken in hand. In February 1738 his friend and patron suddenly died. Luckily he had already introduced him to a number of his own liberal and cultivated friends among whom was Browne Willis, one of the most active in reviving the Society of Antiquaries, and an exceptionally generous patron of learned men and learned institutions. Browne Willis certainly helped and encouraged Hutchins, found him assistants, and finally was instrumental in securing him the living of Wareham in 1744. Hutchins thereupon resigned the Melcombe living, but retained Swyre.

Wareham ought to have been the haven where Hutchins would be. But difficulties kept presenting themselves. In the first place it was a stronghold of Dissent: and Hutchins, not by temperament a controversialist, thought it his duty to confront and confound the opposition to the established church. In the second place it was a borough and returned members to Parliament so that the Rector, who hated politics and took no interest in them, felt obliged to support the patron who had appointed him. And when he could escape from these tiresome and uncongenial additions to the regular duties of ministering to a large parish he did not find all the squirearchy of Dorset by any means as co-operative and enthusiastic as Jacob Bancks had been. Letters remained unanswered. Admittance to records was refused. And even those who were more compliant naturally expected their families, their houses, their genealogies and armorial bearings, to take pride of place in the final work. As Robert Douch justly observes in his introduction to the 1973 reprint 'The *History* was written about, and for, the nobility and gentry'.

Of course this had its compensations. To the modern reader the most valuable are the engraved plates of houses and parks supplied by their owners. To the author, no doubt it was their financial liberality which enabled him to record inscriptions and print documents on a scale that is worthy of the great age of record publication in the following century. It was this too that enabled him to take what is now called sabbatical leave for a few months' study of manuscript collections in Oxford and London while paying for a curate to discharge his parochial duties.

Alas, poor Hutchins! The man he had engaged, a young clergyman hitherto employed as a private tutor in a gentleman's family, proved a disaster. Hardly had the Rector settled down to work in the Bodleian before he was informed that his deputy was a Methodist. This soon turned out to be an understatement. He was a madman and had to be confined. Within a year a worse disaster struck. In 1762 Wareham, like so many Dorset towns in the eighteenth century, suffered a serious fire. Hutchins' library was destroyed – he was away from home – and the rectory all but ruined. The lion-hearted Mrs Hutchins had however snatched up the manuscript of the *History* from her husband's desk and stood in the river, holding it on her head, until the danger had passed. But what such a check must have meant to a man whose particular talent lay in compiling and arranging material, as his friend and biographer claims for him, only those who have so laboured can imagine.

In this dark time his daughter, Anne Martha, came to her father's assistance, acting as his amanuensis. This function became more than ever necessary when he suffered a paralytic stroke in 1771. His physical disabilities had long diminished his effectiveness both as a parish priest and as a historian. He was deaf and suffered from gout. His voice had become so feeble that his parishioners complained that they could not hear his sermons. Only his eyesight and his will-power remained unimpaired.

To the ministrations of his wife and daughter was added the timely reinforcement of the last but not the least of his patrons, Richard Gough. Gough was an even more generous and energetic antiquary than Browne Willis, who had died in 1760, and much more practical. It was largely thanks to him that the whole vast enterprise had been brought to the verge of publication when Hutchins died in June 1773, the very month in which he dates his dedication. The book came out in two folio volumes in 1774 and was widely acclaimed. It sold out almost immediately and a second edition was put in hand.

Wisely it was decided to expand the two stout folios to four of a more manageable size. But Hutchins' death had not appeased the malignancy of the fates towards his work. Fire, this time at the printer's warehouse rather than the rectory at Wareham, destroyed nearly all of the second and third volumes and of course delayed publication. Once again, however, Hutchins' womenfolk came to his rescue. Anne Martha, by now in her early thirties, had been courted by an officer in the East India Company's service. Nearly two years after her father's death she sailed for Bombay where she married him. It was an extremely happy marriage and she bore him one daughter and five sons, all of whom survived infancy, no mean feat in the India of those days. Her husband rose rapidly in his profession and became Commander in Chief, Bombay. With the wealth thus acquired he financed the second edition, a touching tribute of conjugal affection and of respect for his father-in-law.

On this romantic note let us leave the story of this monumental work. The story does not end there but the reader's patience may and Robert Douch's introduction will satisfy any curiosity remaining on the subject. The book is the quintessence of Dorset. In its large, unhurried, well-printed pages we catch the authentic flavour of the county: its quietness, its continuity, its unobtrusive but strong links with the wider history of the country and with England's development as a maritime and imperial power. How appropriate that the money to keep it going when it might have foundered should have been earned in the East India service.

Two other works, one of literary, the other of architectural interest, may be mentioned. *The Hardy Guides* were first published in 1913 and have been reissued by Penguin Books in a most attractive boxed set. They were written by Hermann Lea in close co-operation with Hardy himself. Lea was an enthusiastic and skilful photographer as well as a friend of the author. He lived all his long life – he died in his eighties in 1952 – in Wessex and few, perhaps only Hardy himself, can have had a more intimate knowledge of its topography. Obviously, too obviously, there have been changes since his time. But the new edition provides modern maps and the necessary elucidation with the minimum of fuss. Best of all it reproduces, in abundance, the photographs the author took at the time. Simply as a portrayal of Dorset as it was the books are fascinating. As an account of the visual and topographical sources that nourished Hardy's imagination they are unrivalled.

Last a word must be said about the elegant and charming publications of the Dorset Historic Churches Trust. Entitled simply *Dorset Churches*, the edition of 1988, the fourth, is still in print and often to be found for sale in the churches themselves, generally alongside a more detailed pamphlet describing the particular church you happen to be in. Each edition is delightful: fresh, well illustrated and admirably brief. The standard set by Sir Owen Morshead in the original edition of 1975 is a challenge to any writer. It has certainly stimulated his successors.

XVI
Errors and Omissions

The errors with which this book no doubt shames its author are unintentional and will, if pointed out, be corrected in future editions should an exasperated public call for one. The omissions, on the other hand, are what give it whatever interest it may be found to possess. *L'art d'ennuyer, c'est l'art de tout dire.* The admirable works which I have listed in the previous chapter do not, with the possible exception of Hutchins, set out to be exhaustive. Their authors all leave out a great deal that they could tell us if tact and sense did not restrain them. They wish to please and not to bore. Yet in supplying a comprehensive gazetteer they do tell the reader something about everywhere, even if it is only a polite line or two signifying its virtually total lack of interest or attraction.

The fact that they have done so has been my warrant for the cavalier neglect of places I do not know or only faintly recall. I have visited, and greatly enjoyed visiting, a large number of such places during the writing of this book. But nearly always there was some reason in my mind to suggest that I would find something to interest or delight, which I might communicate to my readers. Idiosyncrasy was the quality emphasised by the publisher and the general editor: and that is the horse I have put my shirt on.

> What man of sense
> My right can doubt
> To put things in
> Or leave things out?

It's done now. But always at such moments of finality one is assailed by self-questioning. Why have I said nothing about charmingly remote places like Compton Valence or its tiny neighbour Compton Abbas, which I know well enough from signposts and may even, years ago when house-hunting, have sneaked a look at? Using these two as a kind of *sortes Virgilianae* let us look them up and see what the experts say.

Well, remoteness and the beauty remoteness confers is about the long and short of it. Both Jo Draper and Michael Pitt-Rivers lay stress on this, though both mention, as of course do John Newman/Nikolaus Pevsner, the nineteenth-century restoration of the parish church at Compton Valence. The last two as architectural historians *par excellence*, draw attention to the unusual features of the restoration and venture, on the strength of them, the opinion that 'Compton Valence may turn out to be of more than local significance'. Happy the future research student whose lot falls in so fair a ground. Turning finally to Hutchins who will certainly say something if there is anything to be said we find him mumbling on in Latin for two folio pages transcribed from the Rolls of Parliament in order to establish at what point the lordship of the manor passed from one Norman family to another. He then gives the best part of a page to the pedigree of the Pelham family, that great eighteenth-century political dynasty to whose enormous estates the distant speck of Compton Valence was added, without, so far as one can see, provoking on their part any interest or concern in the affairs of Dorset. As to Compton Abbas, it is simply mentioned by all authorities as forming part of the parish and that is that.

The inhabitants of Compton Valence, having caught their breath at seeing their hide-out exposed to public view in the index, may exhale gratefully at my failure to provide anyone with a motive for breaking in on their solitude. But, it may be urged, topography is not the only department in which this survey is deficient. There is merely a smattering of genealogy. How high the eyebrows of Hutchins and his subscribers would rise at this dereliction. There is little about archaeology and next to nothing about geology. At the beginning of this book I talk airily of the delights that Dorset offers to the hunters of foxes and of butterflies. But what do *I* offer in these branches of human endeavour? Mutterings about wanting their money back may soon become audible.

To have attempted to satisfy these and all the other forms of curiosity which it would be tedious to enumerate would have been presumptuous. I am not a polymath. And to those seeking specialised information I hope I have indicated its most easily accessible sources. But there are other, greater, deficiencies which I must attempt to supply, chief among them the distinctive quality of Dorset life. I have tried to suggest this elusive essence by incidental comment and detail but I suppose I ought to essay some, not definition exactly, but some general statement which may perhaps draw the threads of the book together.

What is it that makes living in Dorset so agreeable? I have no family roots here, and was in fact born and brought up on the wolds of East Yorkshire and then, in my teens, the Thames Valley. The Lincolnshire wolds, and the Northumberland and Border country have long, and still vigorous, family associations for me. I love all these landscapes dearly except perhaps the Thames Valley, whose climate I dislike and whose natural beauties have been, in the fifty or sixty years that I have known it, so much despoiled.

I mention this not out of the always congenial opportunity to talk about oneself but to provide the reader with a perspective against which to assess my evidence.

The great natural advantage which Dorset possesses, apart from the attractions already described in this book, is its climate. Like the landscape, this is usually considered under the division of East and West. East Dorset is on the whole drier, colder in winter, much exposed to piercing east winds, but has generally rather better summers. West Dorset is softer and wetter. Subject to violent south-west winds which certainly make it feel cold enough in winter it is, along its coast at any rate, remarkably free from frost. It is richer in microclimates, perhaps because of its hilly conformation. Villages only a few miles away from each other vary in rainfall and in the consequent fertility of the land. Stretching along the coast, West Dorset is also particularly subject to the fogs and frets that roll in from the Channel. But these are blemishes only on a remarkably agreeable whole.

No doubt it affects not only the character of the landscape but that of its inhabitants. Compared with Yorkshire or Northumberland they are much more forthcoming. Dorset society is not xenophobic or exclusive. Kindness and friendliness are common to all these counties, at least in my experience, but these qualities are more immediately apparent in Dorset people. And they certainly seem more cheerful and ready to enjoy life. In West Dorset, as in the north of Northumberland, much of the soil is poor and people accept hard work and, till a generation ago, hunger and poverty as part of the human condition. The standard of living has of course risen here enormously over the last four or five decades, as it has almost everywhere else in the developed countries, but Dorset is still a part of England where the small farmer and the small businessman work on slender margins and do not expect life to provide a free lunch. There are great houses and great estates but their owners on the whole concentrate their resources on keeping them up properly rather than on conspicuous consumption. With the possible exception of Bournemouth there are no areas of opulence.

Of course life does not stand still. Supermarkets with their vast car parks and the nightmarish squeaks of the mechanical checkouts are taking the place of shops served and patronised by fellow-members of the human race. Trunk roads and dual carriageways – that hideous, genteel linguistic bogosity – are boring into the fabric of this temperate, deliberate, well-mannered county. Who has ever seen a carriage on a dual carriageway? And is not the word 'way', when employed to signify road or street, a sure sign that something unnatural or superfluous has been thrust on people and places that did not want it? Bureaucracy and the motor car have the whip hand. But perhaps their natural opponents will one day give up their prepossession with bats and badgers and turn their attention to the country and the society that grew there. Change indeed there must always be: but it is possible that it might be organic and not imposed from without.

The golden rule in Dorset is not to be in a hurry. The roads are not, except in the case of a few by-passes, designed for it. If you are driving, once you have left a main road, you will spend most of your time in third gear, not top. And that of course is the pace that will enable you to appreciate what you are travelling through. Bicycling is not so rewarding as in some other counties. Dorset is hilly, especially in the west, and often the hedges are high and the lanes deep. Walking on the other hand is wonderful. Rights of way are generally well marked and the views from the many paths that follow the crests of hills enchanting. The Dorset Coast Path offers spectacular beauties.

If you enjoy riding, that is best of all. A horse gives you the extra height needed to see over hedges: you don't have to bother about the mud of a well-watered country or the mess of cows and bullocks: you can see further ahead, hear more, and often come closer to the wildlife in which the county abounds. Without being a horsy county Dorset takes horses for granted. The common assumption that horses are only owned by the well-to-do would not stand exposure to the facts of Dorset life. People like seeing them about. Commercial drivers and private motorists have time for them.

Time is savoured, not grudged, in Dorset. Unless something forbids it people always stop to exchange conversation when they meet. Yet social life is not demanding. You are perfectly free to go, or not to go, to coffee mornings and the rest of it. It won't be held against you if you don't. But formal courtesies are natural and thus expected.

Thomas Fuller, that large-minded, genial Dorset rector who compiled *The Worthies of England*, treating his subject county

by county, ended each section with a farewell. His valediction
to Dorset reads as follows:

> And now being to take leave of this County I should according to our
> usual manner wish it somewhat for the compleating of its Happiness. But
> it affording in itself all necessities for man's subsistance; and being
> through the conveniency of the Sea supplyed with forraign Commodities,
> I am at a loss what to begge any way additional thereunto.

The wisdom and contentment is characteristic of the county.
May it long so remain.

Index